American Railroads
of the
Nineteenth Century

Entrance gate for passengers, Broad Street Station, Philadelphia, Pennsylvania R.R., 1888.

AMERICAN RAILROADS
OF THE
NINETEENTH CENTURY

A PICTORIAL HISTORY IN
VICTORIAN WOOD ENGRAVINGS

JIM HARTER

TEXAS TECH UNIVERSITY PRESS

This book was set in Times. The paper used in this book meets the minimum requirements of ANSI/NISO Z39.48-1992 (R1997). ∞

Texas Tech University Press
Box 41037
Lubbock, Texas 79409-1037 USA

800-832-4042

ttup@ttu.edu

Http://www.ttup.ttu.edu

Library of Congress Cataloging-in-Publication Data
Harter, Jim.
    American railroads of the nineteenth century : a pictorial history in Victorian wood engravings / written and compiled by Jim Harter.
        p. cm.
    Includes bibliographical references.
    ISBN 0-89672-402-6
    1. Railroad—United States—Pictorial works. 2. Wood engraving, Victorian—United States. I. title.
TF23.H37 1998
385'.0973'022—dc21   98-8400
                                                      CIP

98 99 00 01 02 03 04 05 06 / 9 8 7 6 5 4 3 2 1

CONTENTS

This book is for my brother, Mike Harter, a talented Amarillo, Texas, history teacher, who has an unusual dedication to his students and his community.

It is also dedicated to the memory of our late uncle, Herman "Lee" Harter of Mart, Texas, who for many years was a freight engineer on the Missouri Pacific Railroad.

I would like to acknowledge the following individuals for their contributions to making this book possible: My agent Allan Lang; John and Marty Marmaduke; Ralph and Bennett Kerr; Barbara Harter Whitton; Joan Hall; James Hendricks; Mary LeRoi; John and Joan Digby; Gene Wilde and associates at Miller Blue Print Co. of Austin, Texas; Bill Manning; Don Harold; and my editor, Judith Keeling.

INTRODUCTION

Perhaps as our own century draws to a close, it is a fitting time to look back a hundred years and reflect upon a less complex and more optimistic age. Then, railroads were totally dominant and symbolized the highest technological achievement of their period. Much of the growth and development that occurred in nineteenth-century America could only have happened because of the railroads. Originally developed in England, the steam locomotive was the greatest technological breakthrough in transportation since the discovery of the wheel, freeing mankind at last from thousands of years of dependency on slow-moving, animal-drawn vehicles. Thus railroads were shortly to revolutionize transportation worldwide, drastically cutting its time and cost and making possible a much greater flow of people, goods, and ideas between cities, regions, and countries.

Beginning in America about 1830, railroads slowly and awkwardly began extending outward from East Coast cities. Soon, however, with increasing momentum, they penetrated through mountain barriers into the Mississippi basin, and finally crossed vast distances of hostile western wastelands to the shores of the Pacific. Railroads made possible the rapid settlement of this country, carrying millions of settlers and immigrants to destinations further west, where they rapidly transformed the wilderness into an agriculturally productive part of the nation's economy.

These regions, as well as the South, provided the raw materials for a rapidly expanding industrial economy in the Northeast and Midwest. Railroads, of course, provided the connecting link, bringing in the raw materials and carrying out the manufactured goods. Similarly, the improved transportation offered by local streetcar systems and suburban lines hastened the growth of cities, as workers could live ever greater distances from their places of employment. This nation, which in 1830 was largely rural, divided into regions largely isolated from one another, and given over to primitive types of economic endeavors, had become by 1900 prosperous, dynamic, relatively sophisticated, and a prominent player on the world's stage. It was truly an amazing transformation.

Looking back today, we can see that railroads made possible much that was good, but they also helped to unleash darker forces, which, accelerating in this century, have led to the damaged ecological conditions that prevail over much of our planet. Since 1900 numerous technological developments have occurred, providing many other alternatives to rail transportation. Today we have automobiles, trucks, buses, private planes, jumbo jets; even television and fax machines that "transport" information, people, and goods that a century ago would have moved by rail. One hundred years ago the railroad was indeed king and seemed invincible. How much has changed since that time.

Although the original intention of this book was to provide a good collection of railroad clip art, it soon became obvious that these pictures offer a very special glimpse into that vanished world and should be edited into a form that tells the story of that period with as much richness as possible. To this task my efforts have been dedicated, and I have attempted to organize the material in a way that is chronological but at the same time explores different facets of railroading. Thus, after the first two sections take the reader from the early railroads through the end of the Civil War, the following sections separately examine different aspects of railroading, such as locomotive development from 1865 onward, expansion in the West, railroad stations, passenger service, freight service, horsecar lines, mass transit in New York, and so on. I have also tried to include some obscure aspects of railroading. Among these are a mule-drawn freight line in 1850s Philadelphia, a mining locomotive, a pole-road locomotive, a cog locomotive, horse and steam cars, railroad robberies and train wrecks. There are also images of mass-transit systems and other railroads that were never built, existing only in the minds of eccentric visionaries and in engravings reproduced in the periodicals of the time. Finally, a short introductory text is included at the beginning of each section to give the reader additional historical information and to provide a context for viewing the pictures.

In researching this material, I found no useful engravings published before the early 1850s. About that time the illustrated American periodicals *Ballou's* and *Gleason's,* perhaps following the example of the *Illustrated London News,* began focusing some attention on railroad developments. Both magazines ceased publishing before the Civil War but were replaced by *Harper's Weekly* and *Frank Leslie's Illustrated Newspaper.* These fierce competitors continued coverage on railroads, often focusing with tabloid-like zeal on such sensational events as tragic train accidents. *Scientific American,* in publication since the 1840s, has also contributed many pictures to this book, beginning from the year 1853. Many of the locomotive engravings came from the English periodical *Engineering,* while *Recent Locomotives,* published by *Railroad Gazette,* provided others. Monthly magazines like *Scribner's* and *Harper's Magazine* did some extensive illustrated articles on railroads, and I have included material from these as well. There is much more in this book from other sources too numerous to mention.

Whatever the imperfections of this volume, it should give a fairly accurate depiction of the railroad world of that time, providing rail fans, model railroaders, and other nostalgic individuals with useful historical information and a treasure trove of interesting images, most of which are rare and have never been previously published in book form. All of this material is in the public domain and can be used as clip art.

1 • THE EARLY YEARS

It appears that the idea of railways is a very old one, going all the way back to ancient Greece, where a primitive technology existed in which carts were pushed or drawn between parallel lines of stone slabs. By the sixteenth century, carts with small iron wheels were operated in German mines over rails of wood. Cast-iron rails were developed in the 1770s, and by the year 1800 there were about two hundred miles of horse-drawn railways in England.

Although a number of individuals were experimenting with steam traction, credit for the first steam locomotive is generally attributed to the Englishman Richard Trevithick for his invention built in 1803. Other inventors, among them Blenkinsop, William Hedly, and George Stephenson, were inspired to follow, although they were to encounter many obstacles. By about 1812 development had reached the stage where primitive locomotives began being used on small colliery lines in England.

By this time Americans had also become interested in the possibility of railways. Travel in early nineteenth-century America was frequently difficult and time-consuming. Roads were often little more than old Indian trails or cow paths, and generally more suited to horseback travel than stage or wagon. Cities were much more isolated, and therefore by necessity more self-sufficient. As most were ports, virtually all commerce and travel that did move between them went by water. At this time, as well, there was a strong reluctance on the part of the national and state governments to involve themselves in "internal improvements" such as road building. As a result, private toll roads came into being to partially alleviate the situation. Canal building helped also, but the transportation problem remained immense.

By 1825, Colonel John Stevens, an early promoter of railways, had a small locomotive built that operated on his estate at Hoboken, New Jersey. Later, a few small railways were built, using horses to pull the rail carts or carriages; among them, the Baltimore & Ohio. However, it was George Stephenson's *Rocket,* winning an important English competition in 1829, that finally seemed to convince most people of the real power, practicality, and usefulness of steam engines.

About this same time a small number of locomotives began being tested on American railways. An English engine, the *Stourbridge Lion,* was tested on August 8, 1829, at Honesdale, Pennsylvania, but was too heavy for the track. On August 28, 1830, on the B&O line, American Peter Cooper's *Tom Thumb* was beating a horse in a competition where both were drawing loaded railway carriages. A mechanical failure caused Cooper's locomotive to lose, but it still made its case.

Another American engine, the *Best Friend,* became the first locomotive to pull a train in this country in November 1830, on the Charleston & Hamburg line. The *John Bull,* imported from the Stephenson works in England, was employed on the Camden & Amboy Railroad in 1831. It was shortly fitted with a new American invention, the "cow catcher." Also in 1831, an American-built locomotive, the *De Witt Clinton,* began operating on the Mohawk & Hudson line. This later became the New York Central Railroad.

Following these early years, locomotive builders continued to innovate and rapidly made improvements over existing designs. Firms were set up to build locomotives commercially. The most famous of these manufacturers included the West Point Iron Works; Davis & Gartner in York, Pennsylvania; Stevens' Workshop in Hoboken; and Ross Winans in Balti-

more. In 1836, in a seemingly impossible feat, the *George Washington,* a locomotive built by William Norris of Philadelphia, drew a load of almost ten tons up a 2,800-foot incline that rose one foot in every fourteen. This impressive demonstration attracted some orders for Norris, including one from the Birmingham & Gloucester Railway in England. The Norris Company went on to become involved in the manufacture of steam engines in Austria and influenced locomotive design elsewhere in Europe. For a time it and Baldwin rivaled for dominance in this country; however, the Norris firm was declining by the beginning of the Civil War and went out of business in 1866.

Relatively early, railroads had learned to differentiate between the motive power required for passenger service and that required for freight. Pulling shorter trains of lighter cars, passenger engines were designed to maximize speed, but at the expense of pulling power. Pulling longer trains of heavier cars, freight locomotives were designed with exactly the opposite emphasis. Thus passenger engines had thrusting and connecting rods designed to rotate closer to the hubs of the driving wheels, whereas freight locomotives had them further away. The drivers on passenger engines were larger than those on freight. Freight locomotives, however, often had more drivers, or more added weight on them to give better adhesion.

Early locomotives were built with various wheel configurations, but by the early 1840s it was recognized that the 4-4-0 type had distinct advantages. (This three-number classification given to locomotives indicates the number of front carrying wheels, followed by the drivers, and then the trailers.) In 1837 the first two locomotives of this type were built, and one, the *Hercules,* performed impressively. In 1839, another 4-4-0, the *Gowan and Marx,* hauled a 423-ton train from Reading, Pennsylvania, to Philadelphia. Thomas Rodgers of Paterson, New Jersey, who soon became an important manu- facturer, built his first 4-4-0 in 1844, and Mathias Baldwin built his first in 1845.

The Camden and Amboy Railroad, on the important route between New York and Philadelphia, carried 110,000 passengers its first year of operation, thus demonstrating the commercial potential of railroads. Railroad fever quickly spread through the eastern U.S., with many small lines being chartered, although a financial crisis from 1837 to 1840 slowed things somewhat. Total railroad mileage in 1840 was 3,328; by 1850 it was 8,879; and it reached an impressive 30,626 by 1860.

Perhaps more typical of the railroads built at this time was the Erie & Kalamazoo. The first line to operate in both the states of Ohio and Michigan, it was promoted as the "Pioneer Railroad of the West." Planned initially to extend from Toledo, on Lake Erie, to the Kalamazoo River, it was constructed only to Adrian, Michigan, a distance of thirty-three miles. Laid with four-inch square oak rails, the line was begun in 1835 and opened on October 3, 1836. Originally horse traction was employed, but soon iron straps were nailed over the wooden rails, and by June 1837, a locomotive was in use. The "Pleasure Car," a twenty-four-seat passenger coach of rather whimsical design, was added shortly thereafter. Operating conditions on the line were slowly improved, but by 1842, financial difficulties resulted in seizure of the company property by the local sheriff. Subsequently the line became a part of the Michigan Southern Railroad.

Although perhaps an improvement over stage travel, early train rides still were not so pleasant. Speed was improved, but sparks from the engine could burn one's clothing, skin, or hair. There was little or no ballast under the tracks, and rides were bumpy, curves were sharp, and derailments too frequent. Early cars were often open to the elements. Carriages adapted for rail were later replaced with long wooden cars that had no springs. These typically had long bench seats with no backs, running the width of the car. Springs, middle aisles, and seat backs came shortly later. Train delays were frequent also, for a number of reasons. The introduction of telegraphic dispatching in 1851 helped to improve things, but it was many years before all rail lines had adopted this system.

Besides being uncomfortable, train rides could be dangerous. A black fireman on the *Best Friend* became the first recorded railroad fatality when a boiler exploded. On August 11, 1837, the first rail collision with fatalities occurred on the Portsmouth & Roanoke line near Suffolk, Virginia. Yet in the early years fatalities were amazingly few—primarily because the speeds were slow, the traffic light, and little movement took place at night. In 1853 America was shocked when an accident took a record twenty-one lives, and even more shocked two weeks later when a head-on collision at Secaucus, New Jersey, claimed forty-six more. This initiated a new, disturbing trend in railway tragedies that was to haunt the nation for many years to come.

As virtually all the capital available to the early railroads was tied up in track, bridges, and equipment; stations were not a priority. Any convenient building would usually suffice, and sometimes nearby taverns or general stores would take on the added chore. Stations, when they were built, were usually of wood, had no platform, and consisted basically of a house for the use of the stationmaster and a storage shed. The most primitive stations were unmanned platforms, which would have a signaling device for use by anyone wishing to board a train.

The first railroad station built as such was the Mt. Clare Station in Baltimore, on the B&O line, in 1830. The first B&O station in Washington, D.C., was located in the rear of a tailor shop. One early station, built in Lowell, Massachusetts, in 1835, adapted a classical Greek temple style and had a track laid through a colonnade. A number of brick stations were built in Boston rather early. Among these, the Old Colony Station, built in 1847, and later known as the Kneeland Street Station, stood out. It had on its premises a newsstand, barber shop, bootblack's stand, telegraph office, lady's salon, smoking room, and general waiting room.

In 1848 an impressive station was built at New Haven, Connecticut, in the Italian villa style, by the architect Henry Austin. This may have inspired other railroads. Shortly, as their prosperity increased, some lines began to compete in the magnificence of their big-city terminals. By the late 1850s, many fine structures were being built. Typically, these incorporated eclectic mixes of various architectural styles, and usually featured, in the fashion of the time, two towers for added decoration.

In the 1850s the longer and leaner 4-4-0s, now known as the American type, were being built in far greater numbers than any other variety of engine. Leaving behind their less attractive ancestors, these locomotives were lavished with artistic attention: they were colorfully painted, had fixtures of polished brass and cabs of finished hardwood, were detailed with miniature paintings and other ornamentation, and given exotic names displayed in beautiful lettering. In the largely rural America of that time, these locomotives represented the romance of big cities and faraway places—a connection to a much larger world.

As the year 1860 approached, train travel was beginning to seem civilized. The many isolated short lines often had grown and connected with each other. Roadbeds had improved and equipment had become more sophisticated and comfortable. Trains ran more often, on better-kept schedules, and with a little more speed. The Alleghenies had been crossed and rails now extended to cities like Chicago, and even over to the Mississippi. In the larger stations one might now find magazines, newspapers, cigars, food, and other goods and services available.

The country was slowly being connected by railroads in a way that was bringing it closer together on many new levels. Yet, other winds were blowing. The unfinished issues of states' rights and slavery divided the nation and had to be resolved. The American Civil War was at hand.

Early European steam: Top left; "Puffing Billy" as rebuilt in 1815. Top right; George Stephenson. Middle left; Cugnot's road vehicle, 1767. Middle right; Locomotive "Agenoria," Shutt End Ry., 1829. Bottom left; Stephenson's Killingsworth engine, 1816. Bottom right; Stephenson's "Rocket," 1829.

Early American railroads: Top; The "De Witt Clinton," Mohawk Valley R.R., 1831. Upper middle: Left; Early passenger coach. Center; First passenger car drawn by horse, Baltimore & Ohio R.R., 1829. Right; Passenger train, Erie & Kalamazoo R.R., 1837. Lower middle: Left; The "South Carolina," 1831. Center; The "Best Friend," 1830. Right; The "West Point," 1830. Bottom; The "De Witt Clinton," 1831.

Early American railroads: Top left; The "Grasshopper," Baltimore & Ohio R.R., 1834. Top right; The "John Bull" after 1836 modification, Camden & Amboy R.R. Upper center; Boston and Worcester R.R. train, 1835. Lower center; Early train. Middle right; Peter Cooper's "Tom Thumb," B. & O. R.R., 1830. Bottom; Trial run of the "De Witt Clinton," 1831.

13

Early American locomotives: Top left; William James' "James I," B. & O. R.R., 1832. Top right; John Jervis' "Experiment," the world's first engine with front truck or bogie, Mohawk & Hudson R.R., 1832. Middle left; Henry R. Campbell's "Campbell," Philadelphia, Germanstown & Norriston R.R., 1837. Middle right; William Norris' "Lafayette," B. & O. R.R., 1837. Bottom left; Ross Winans' "Mazeppa," B. & O. R.R., 1837. Bottom right; Ross Winans' "Buffalo," B. & O. R.R., 1844.

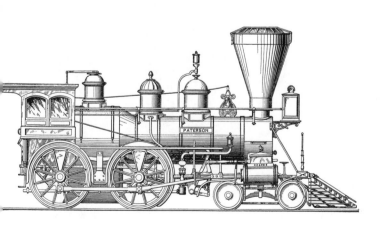

The evolution of early American locomotives: Top left; The "Best Friend," 1830. Top right; The "West Point," 1830. Middle left; Rogers 4-4-0 "American" type passenger engine, Hartford & New Haven R.R., 1845. Middle right; 4-4-0 express engine, Hudson River R.R., 1849. Bottom left; Rogers 4-4-0 passenger engine, 1853. Bottom right; Rogers 2-6-0 "Mogul" type freight engine, New Jersey R.R., 1863.

6-2-0 Crampton style engine built by Norris & Son, Camden & Amboy R.R., 1849.

Top; Amoskeag 4-4-0 "American" type engine, 1856. Middle; Norris 4-4-0 passenger engine, 1854. Bottom; Norris 4-6-0 "Ten Wheeler" type freight engine, 1854.

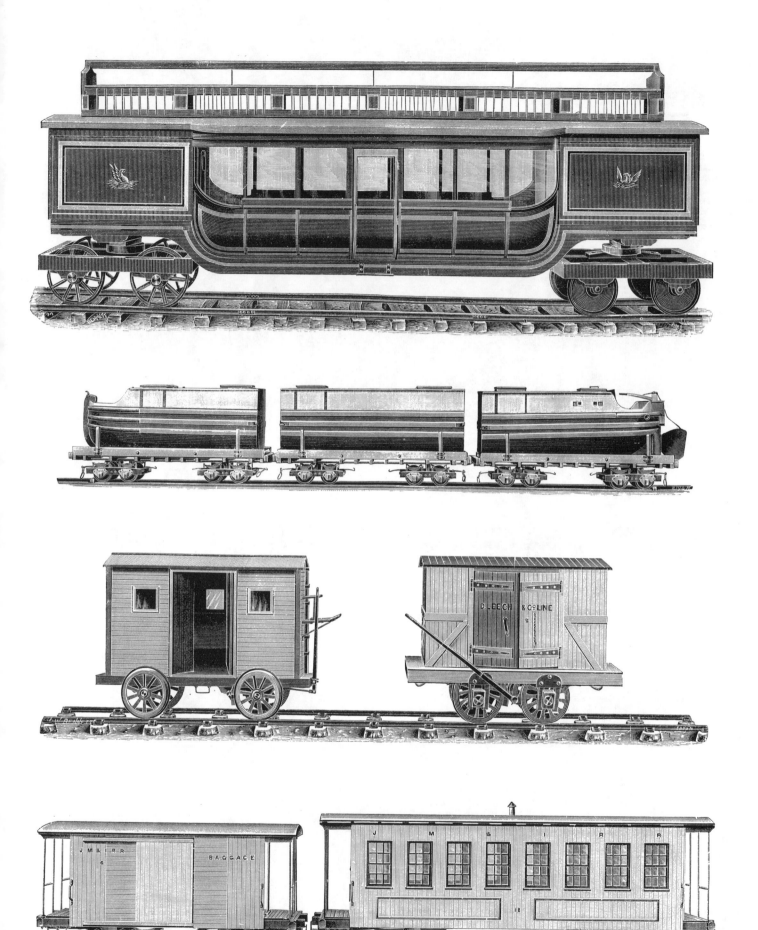

Early American rolling stock: Top; First bogie passenger car, Pennsylvania R.R., 1834. Upper middle; Sectional canal boat and cars, Alleghany Portage R.R., 1843. Lower middle: Left; Passenger car, Portage R.R., 1834. Right; Freight car, Portage R.R., 1835. Bottom; Freight car and passenger car, Jeffersonville, Madison & Indianapolis R.R., 1848.

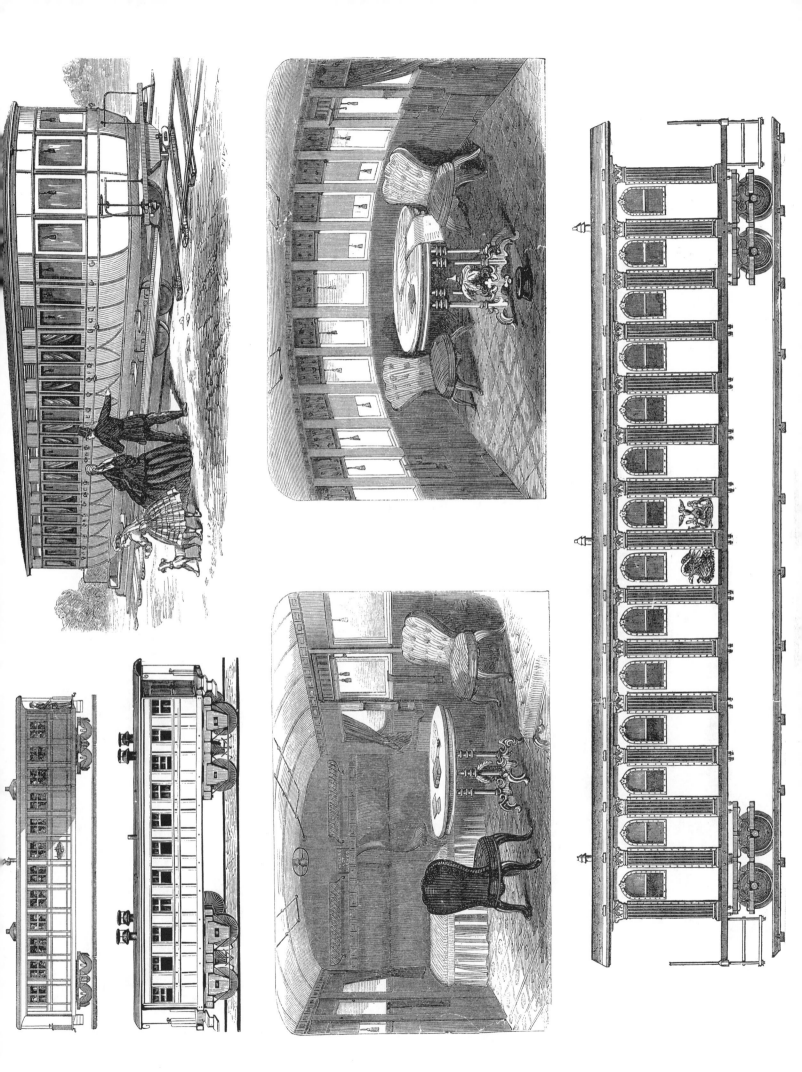

Early passenger cars: Top left; Car, 1834. Top right; English car imported for use by Old Colony R.R., c.1854. Upper middle left; Early car. Lower middle: Left; Rear compartment of Old Colony car. Right; Front compartment of Old Colony car. Bottom; Typical passenger car, c.1853.

Horses would draw cars through Manhattan to pick up passengers for trips to New England. Top; Detaching the horses, New York & New Haven R.R., 1852. Bottom; Cars being drawn up at 32nd St. and 4th Avenue to be hooked to locomotive, early 1850s.

Top; Interior of passenger car, New York & New Haven R.R., 1852. Bottom; Interior of passenger car, Baltimore & Ohio R.R., 1861.

Top; Train ascending the Alleghenies between Harrisburg and Pittsburg, Pennsylvania R.R., 1853. Middle; Passenger train, Worcester, Mass., 1852. Bottom; Locomotive with Massachusetts State Prison in background, 1858.

Top; Departure of the legislative train at Albany for New York, Hudson River R.R., c.1855. Bottom; Railroad scene, Somerville, Mass., Boston & Lowell R.R., 1853.

Top; Train at depot, Yonkers, N.Y., 1858. Middle; The inauguration of the Ohio & Mississippi R.R., Chilicothe, Ohio, 1857. Bottom; Train at Anthony's Nose, Mohawk River, N.Y., New York Central R.R., 1857.

Top; Passing trains meet at Albany, N.Y., Hudson River R.R., 1859. Bottom; Arrival of the first train at Jamestown, N.Y., Atlantic and Great Western R.R., 1860.

Top left; Engine houses at Rochester, N.Y., Niagara R.R., 1855. Top right; Locomotive on turn table, c.1855. Middle left; Passenger train of 1850s. Middle right; Train at station, c.1860. Bottom; Passenger train of 1850s.

Top; Early sleeping car, New York Central R.R., 1859. Bottom; "Waiting for the Train," 1858.

Top; Interior of depot at Worcester, Mass., 1854. Bottom; Train at Ohio & Mississippi R.R. depot, Cincinnati, 1857.

Top; Southern & Western R.R. station, at Broad and Prime Streets, Philadelphia, 1853. Middle left; New York Central depot, Rochester, 1855. Middle right; View in rear of depot, Jersey City, N.J., 1855. Bottom; North side of Great Central Depot, Illinois Central and Michigan Central railroads, Chicago, 1857.

Top; South side of Great Central Depot, Illinois Central and Michigan Central railroads, Chicago, 1856. Bottom; Railroad stations in Boston, 1856.

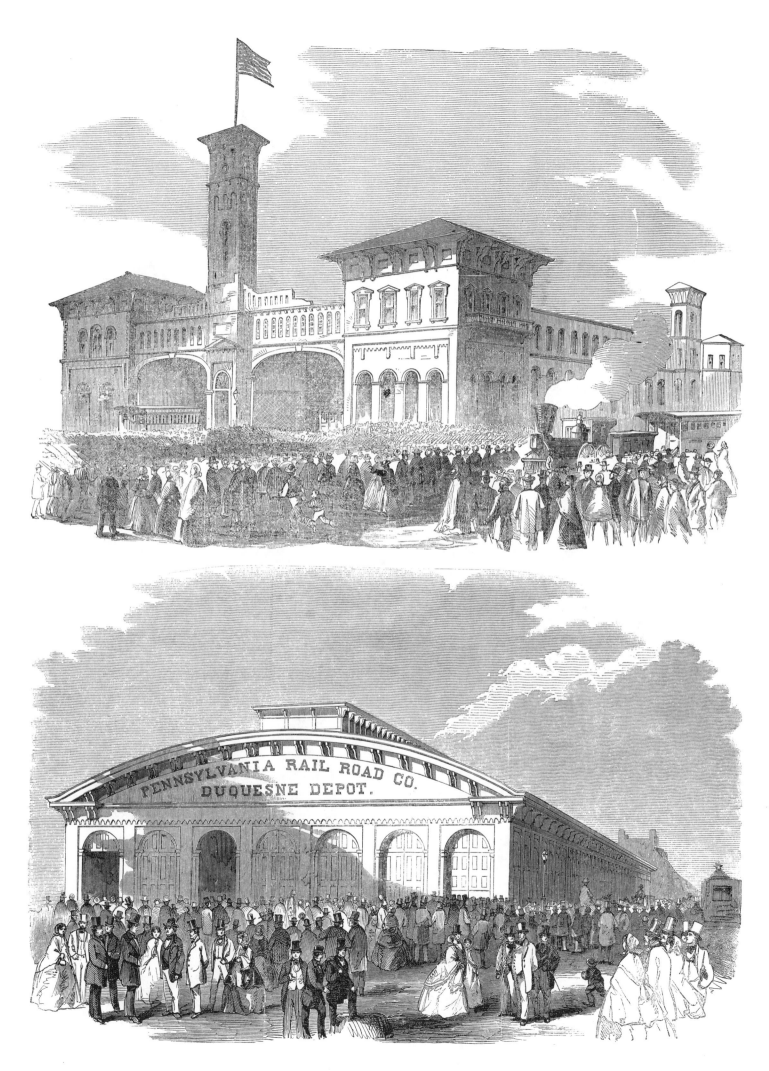

Top; Pennsylvania R.R. depot at Harrisburg, 1862. Bottom; P.R.R. depot on site of Fort Duquesne, Pittsburgh, 1858.

Richard Norris & Son's Locomotive Works, Philadelphia, 1855.

Top; Bridge near Colona, Ill., Chicago, Rock Island & Pacific R.R., 1857. Bottom; Bridge over Raritan River, Central Railroad of New Jersey, 1854.

Top; Bridge over Green River, Louisville & Nashville R.R., 1855. Bottom; Covered bridge, with bow truss in center, over Cumberland River at Nashville, L & N. R.R., 1862.

Top; Early snow plow used at Wellington Hill depot near Boston, 1856. Bottom; Train in a snow storm, 1859.

Top; Early train wreck near Paterson, N.J., New York & Erie R.R., 1853. Bottom; Raising the cars after a wreck in New Jersey, 1857.

Top; Bridge collapse takes 20 lives, Ohio & Mississippi R.R., 1861. Bottom; Passenger car derailment, New York & Erie R.R., July 1858.

2 - RAILROADS IN THE CIVIL WAR

In 1860, when the conflict between North and South was fast approaching, there was a distinct contrast in the railroad systems of the two regions. The North, which was more populous and economically integrated, had a much larger and more complete network over its area. That of the rural South was rather primitive and fragmented, and its supply of locomotives and rolling stock compared even worse. There was a diversity of gauge sizes on southern lines that usually prevented the equipment of one railroad from running on the tracks of another. That year total miles of track in the North were reported to be 20,814, and 9,819 in the South. The three southern states of Texas, Louisiana, and Arkansas had a collective total of only about 700 miles.

The four main cities along the North's eastern coast, Boston, New York, Philadelphia, and Baltimore, all had rail links penetrating through the mountains and connecting into the Midwest. The South, by comparison, had only one such line, the Memphis and Charleston, which went through the Blue Ridge Mountains. It is interesting, and perhaps symbolic, that there was no direct rail connection anywhere between North and South. There were about a dozen manufacturers of locomotives in the North, whereas the single one in the South was diverted to making military hardware once the war began. Rail manufacturing was all done in the North as well.

Although England built a military line to support the siege of Sebastapol in the Crimean War, and France made some use of railways in the Austro-Sardinian conflict of 1859, railroads were still a largely unknown factor in the art of making war. However, this was not to be for long. On April 18, 1861, just days after the first shelling of Fort Sumter, a Confederate militia led by Captain John D. Imbolden led an attack involving movement over three rail lines, which resulted in the capture of Harper's Ferry, Virginia. This town, situated on the Potomac River, was a strategic point on the Baltimore & Ohio Railroad. This railroad, as well as others like the Louisville & Nashville, the Orange & Alexandria, and the Manassas Gap, all existed in contended areas that changed hands a number of times over the next few years. As railroads were used by commanders to ferry troops and supplies in an effort to gain advantage over their opponents, it quickly became a primary war objective to defend one's own tracks, equipment, bridges, tunnels, stations, and junction points while destroying those of the opponent. Thus these contended rail lines were periodically battered and then patched together a number of times in the years that followed.

Confederate general Stonewall Jackson displayed an early brilliance in using railroads to his own advantage. On May 23, 1861, by a clever ruse, Jackson was able to capture fifty-six locomotives and over three hundred cars at Harper's Ferry. A few lighter locomotives and some cars were sent to Winchester and later moved by teams over roads to the nearest southern line. The rest he removed to Martinsburg, but was forced to burn when he withdrew. At the first battle of Bull Run, General Beauregard had Joseph E. Johnston's troops transported by train from the Winchester area, where they joined the battle, already in progress, and decisively affected its outcome. Later the Confederate cavalry leaders Forrest, Stuart, and Mosby were to show considerable skill in disabling railroads behind enemy lines.

Although the North had clear railroad superiority, its capital, Washington, D.C., ironically, was in the position of being more vulnerable than that of its opponent, Richmond, Virginia. Washington was served by a single rail line, the B&O, which went to Baltimore. Richmond was served by four lines. Following President Lincoln's request for troops early in the war, a great mass of soldiers moved by rail from all over the North toward Washington. They all had to go through Baltimore, a city with many southern sympathizers; arriving at one station and marching through town to embark at another. Early troop movements there quickly aroused resentment and mob violence. Lincoln was in a delicate position, as he did not wish to alienate Baltimore and the state of Maryland from the cause of the Union. The situation was not resolved for some days, but finally the troops arrived in Washington.

Lincoln also had problems with his secretary of war, Simon Cameron, a figure of controversy whose family controlled the Northern Central Railroad. Cameron forcefully argued for a hard-line position in the Baltimore crisis but lost out. He arrogantly controlled situations in such a way as to favor the business of his own line and that of the Pennsylvania Railroad, to the detriment of others, especially the B&O. It was some time before he was replaced, however.

The South demonstrated an early genius for the destruction of railroads, but the North, in turn, showed an early capacity for quickly rebuilding them. A real hero in this effort was Herman Haupt, former chief engineer of the Pennsylvania Railroad, and perhaps one of the foremost railroad construction engineers of the world. He was originally recruited in early 1862 by General McDowell to repair a line near Fredericksburg, Virginia. With a group of untrained volunteers, having only hand tools and laboring in cold, rainy weather, he built a span over Potomac Creek, four hundred feet long and one hundred feet high, in twelve days. The previous bridge had required a year to construct. This feat drew the attention of President Lincoln, and Colonel Haupt soon gained other responsibilities. What slowly evolved under him was the Construction Corps, which eventually employed about seventeen thousand at its maximum strength. The Corps assumed responsibility for repairing, operating, and maintaining Union-controlled railroads while destroying those of the enemy. Brigadier General Haupt was later replaced by Brigadier General Daniel McCallum, and Haupt returned to civilian life.

In 1862, James J. Andrews, a Union spy, and General Ormsby M. Mitchell hatched a bizarre scheme to capture Chattanooga, Tennessee. A part of the plot involved Andrews leading a group to capture a Confederate train near Marietta, Georgia, and then taking it north toward Chattanooga, sabotaging rail facilities along the way. Cut off from the South, Chattanooga would then be in a much more vulnerable position. Andrews, and a party of twenty, traveled incognito in small groups and seized the locomotive *General* along with three cars at Big Shanty. They made rapid progress until being delayed at Kingston for some time.

Meanwhile W. A. Fuller, the train conductor, and Jeff Cain, the engineer, took off in pursuit using a handcar. They found an old locomotive and continued on to Kingston. There they took a newer locomotive and gave chase once more. On encountering a broken rail they abandoned the locomotive and ran on to find another one. Taking the *Texas,* they pursued at speeds of up to 60 MPH, rapidly closing the gap. Andrew's train released two cars to delay the pursuit, but they were running low on fuel. Finally the last car was set afire and left blazing on a wooden bridge. The *Texas* was able to push the burning car ahead to a siding and then continued on. Having run out of fuel, Andrews and most of his men were captured. Later Andrews and seven others were hung.

The heroism of Fuller and Cain typified the heroic efforts of many others to keep the trains running. Many rail employees on both sides of the conflict suffered through hunger and lack of sleep and were often victims in sabotage attempts. Hundreds of engineers and firemen perished from sniper fire, derailments, and train accidents.

Although the North was able to replace its trains and train crews, the South did not find it so easy. Perhaps because of either an overconcern for "states' rights" or merely the incompetence of its officials, a clear railroad policy was never developed. Railroads were largely left to their own resources, yet they did the best they could under the circumstances. The demands of the war rapidly deteriorated their lines and equipment and exhausted their reserve stocks of rails and repair parts. There was a severe manpower shortage as well. Ultimately less important lines had to be cannibalized to provide rails to maintain the other ones. This continual decline resulted in ever-increasing shortages of supplies and diminished troop mobility.

Despite this, General Longstreet, following the defeat at Gettysburg, made a daring maneuver when he moved his troops from one theater of operations to another. This journey involved going through Richmond, Wilmington, Augusta, and Atlanta to detrain at Ringgold, Georgia, twenty-two miles south of Chattanooga. It required crossing over ten railroads to cover the almost one thousand miles. Luckily, his troops arrived just in time to save the battle of Chickamauga for the Confederacy. Shortly thereafter, "Fighting Joe" Hooker brought his Union troops by train across the mountains to fight in Tennessee as well.

In contrast to those in the South, railroads in the North had prospered. Business had boomed, and both military and civilian traffic, passenger and freight, moved relatively unimpeded. New locomotives, cars, and rails were being rapidly manufactured and just as quickly utilized in the expanding war effort. Now much of this material found its way to Tennessee.

In 1864 General William T. Sherman left Chattanooga, beginning his march to Atlanta. He cleverly avoided fighting General Johnston in situations favorable to the Confederates, instead outflanking them and continually cutting the rail lines behind them. Thus Johnston was forced to retreat all the way to Atlanta, where he was replaced by General Hood. In his advance, Sherman received constant support from the Construction Corps, which repaired the rails behind him, maintaining the all-important supply line. Their bridging of the Chattahoochee River was considered the foremost engineering feat of the war. Union troops cut all rail lines to Atlanta and the city was forced to surrender. Sherman continued his march to Savannah, destroying two railroads along the way.

General Grant's strategy in the east involved cutting off all the rail lines to Richmond and Petersburg, just as Sherman did in Atlanta. In this he was successful, and General Lee was finally forced to surrender at Appomattox. The strategic importance of railroads in war had been powerfully demonstrated, as were cleverly executed tactics to disable or destroy them. There would be new ideas for military men of the world to ponder. Railroads in the North were stronger than ever before, but it would take many years for those in the South to recover.

Top; Battery of Massachusetts artillerymen protecting route of Baltimore & Ohio R.R., at Relay House near Harper's Ferry, May 1861. Bottom; Destruction by rebels of B. & O. bridge over Potomac River, Harper's Ferry, June 15, 1861.

Fiery hay loaded cars pulled onto bridge, Harper's Ferry, June 15, 1861.

41

Gen. Robert C. Schenck, with 1st Regiment, Ohio Volunteers, fired into by a masked battery near Vienna, Va., Alexandria, Loudoun & Hampshire R.R., June 17, 1861.

Railroad battery devised for protecting workmen while rebuilding burned bridges on both the Baltimore & Ohio and Philadelphia, Wilmington, & Baltimore Railroads, 1861.

Top; Western & Atlantic R.R. locomotive "General," seized in Andrew's raid of 1862. Middle; Confederates destroying track by twisting rails. Bottom; Baltimore & Ohio locomotives destroyed by Gen. Stonewall Jackson's troops at Martinsburg, Va., 1861.

Top; View of track through swamps, Charleston & Savannah R.R., 1862. Bottom; Resin, cotton, and turpentine being loaded in Union-occupied Fernandina, Fla., for shipment to New York, Florida R.R., 1862. This 5 ft. gauge, 156 mile line, also called "Yulee's Railroad" after its builder, connected Fernandina on the Atlantic with Cedar Key on the Gulf. Although both ports were captured early, the Confederacy continued to operate the line in the interior.

Top; Brig. Gen. Jeb Stuart's Confederate cavalry firing into train near Turnstall's Station, Va., Richmond & York River R.R., June 13, 1862. Bottom; Intersection of Orange & Alexandria R.R. with Manassas Gap R.R. at Manassas Junction, Va., Mar. 1862.

Top; Intersection of Memphis & Charleston R.R. with Mississippi & Ohio R.R. at Grand Junction, Tenn., late 1862. Bottom; Station at Stevenson, Ala., held by Union forces, Aug. 1862. This town was the converging point for the Nashville & Chattanooga, Memphis & Charleston, and the Tennessee & Georgia Railroads.

Top; Confederate freight train, Petersburg, Va., late 1862. Bottom; President Lincoln's visit to the Army of the Potomac, arrival at Frederick, Md., Baltimore & Ohio R.R., autumn 1862.

Falmouth Station, chief supply depot of the Army of the Potomac; Richmond, Fredericksburg & Potomac R.R., early 1863.

Five locomotives, built from scrap by Union forces at captured Vicksburg, 1863. These were probably intended for use on the Southern Mississippi R.R.

Occupation of Wrightsville, Pa. by Gen. Robert E. Lee's army and destruction of the railway bridge over the Susquehanna by Union forces, Columbia R.R., June 28, 1863.

Top; Burning of the Rappahannock railway bridge by Union forces; Richmond, Fredericksburg & Potomac R.R., Oct. 13, 1863. Bottom; The great depot of supplies for the Army of the Potomac, Oct. 1863.

Top; Union hospital train operating on Nashville & Chattanooga R.R., early 1864. Bottom; Interior of a hospital car.

Scenes on the Western & Atlantic R.R. in Georgia during Gen. Sherman's march to Atlanta: Top; Gen. Logan's troops at Big Shanty station, June 10, 1864. Bottom; Installing military telegraph alongside rail line at Ackworth, June 1864.

Top; Confederate incursion into Maryland: Capture of a train on the Baltimore & Ohio R.R., Magnolia, Md., July 11, 1864. Bottom; Destruction of railroad equipment by Gen. Hood prior to Confederate evacuation of Atlanta, Sept. 2, 1864.

Top; Union troop train in Virginia exposed to rebel fire from Cemetery Hill, Sept. 1864. Bottom; Union military railroad outside of Petersburg, Va., Oct. 1864.

Top; Gen. Warren's raid on Weldon R.R. Destruction of water tanks at Jarret's Station, late 1864. Middle; Arrival of Union recruits during fight at Peeble farm, Sept. 30, 1864. Bottom; View in Atlanta after Union occupation, Nov. 1864.

3 · AMERICAN LOCOMOTIVES: 1865-1900

In 1863, the Pennsylvania Railroad began the replacement of iron rails on its line with new ones made of steel. At a time when the energies of the nation were being consumed in a struggle for its very existence, this event attracted little attention. However, it was significant, as it made possible the creation of larger and more powerful engines than had previously been available. This revolution did not take place all at once, but gradually and in small increments. Yet, by the end of the century locomotive technology had tremendously changed, and in so doing, had benefited the growth and prosperity of the nation.

One early change, following the Civil War, was the conversion of most wood-fueled engines to use cleaner-burning coal. Coal had been used for fuel by a few Pennsylvania lines as early as the 1830s, but transportation costs and primitive mining techniques made it too expensive for lines outside the mining regions. In time, however, firewood became scarcer and costlier and coal cheaper and more abundant. This adjustment led to a change in locomotive design, as the "funnel" stacks, needed to trap sparks and cinders, were no longer necessary.

Though the popular 4-4-0 locomotives were often used for freight, after 1865 they were increasingly relegated to passenger service. The 4-6-0 Ten Wheeler type, introduced by Norris in 1847, was found to be ideal for freight and by the Civil War had gained wide acceptance, largely replacing older 0-6-0 and 0-8-0 designs. In 1863, the 2-6-0 Mogul type was introduced as a freight engine. This was followed by the heavier 2-8-0 Consolidation in 1866, and yet more massive 2-10-0 Decapod in 1867.

During this same period improvements were also made in locomotive safety. In 1866 a safety valve was developed that would automatically release steam pressure once it reached a dangerous level. Also that year the Pennsylvania Railroad began the exclusive use of steel in the manufacture of boiler sheets and tubes on its locomotives. This made possible the building of engines for operation at higher levels of steam pressure. In 1869 George Westinghouse invented an air-pressure braking system. A few years later Lovett Eames developed a vacuum braking system. The Westinghouse system gradually gained nationwide acceptance, but both allowed for the operation of trains at higher speeds and with greater safety.

For years, most railroad companies had manufactured at least some of their own locomotives. In 1868, the Central Pacific, which had previously purchased engines in the East and shipped them around Cape Horn, began its own manufacture in Sacramento. As time passed, locomotive manufacturing changed, requiring newer and heavier machines, larger buildings, and more operating capital. Some companies, like Baldwin and Rogers, became much bigger, while others just survived, or eventually failed.

In one interesting innovation, around 1877, the Wootten boiler and firebox was developed for using the harder, slower-burning anthracite coal. In this system, an improvement over earlier anthracite-fueled models, the engineer's cab was moved forward toward the center of the locomotive, where it sat straddling the boiler. This made possible a larger combustion chamber in the rear to facilitate the burning process. Stationed there in the back to shovel the coal, the fireman received little protection from the weather. Also called Camelback or Mother Hubbard, this type of engine was mainly used on the anthracite lines like the Reading, Lehigh Valley, and Lackawanna.

The 4-4-0 reached its peak year of production in 1872, but remained popular until the end of the century. Although it had a number of shortcomings, many ingenious innovations were devised to improve its performance. It was built heavier for better adhesion and designed to operate at higher levels of steam pressure. Also by this time passenger trains were becoming longer and the cars heavier. In 1891 the New York Central built a 4-4-0 weighing sixty tons. In 1893 the line's *Number 999,* also a heavy 4-4-0, pulled the *Empire State Express* 112.5 MPH, setting a famous speed record. Even later, one weighing sixty-eight tons and having forty-five tons on the drivers was tested, but was found too heavy for the track.

In 1886 the first 4-6-2 "Pacific," a type later to become popular as a passenger engine, was built at the Wilkes Barre shops of the Lehigh Valley R.R. In 1888 the 4-4-2 "Atlantic" type was introduced. By 1895 these Atlantics began to replace many 4-4-0 passenger locomotives. In 1889 Baldwin built the first American compound locomotives. Having multiple cylinders, these engines used less fuel and water and were favored for freight use on lines with steep grades. This technology was shortly adapted for speed as well, but improvements on the superheater system, about 1900, made compound technology obsolete.

From 1865 to 1900 locomotives would be adapted for many other specialized purposes. On July 3, 1869, the world's first cog railroad inaugurated its service at Mount Washington, New Hampshire, on a line having very steep grades. For this purpose small cog locomotives, with vertical boilers, were built. Many other small engines were manufactured and used for switching, for carrying passengers on elevated or suburban lines, in industrial situations, and for mining, logging, and agricultural purposes. Many of these were built from the designs of Matthew N. Forney, a noted mechanical engineer and author of the widely used handbook *Catechism of the Locomotive.* For other logging operations, the more primitive pole road locomotives were built. These had flanged wheels and ran over lines of joined wooden poles. Many other American-built engines were exported to Latin America, Australia, Asia, and elsewhere.

At the turn of the century America had approximately 193,000 miles of track over which operated about forty thousand steam engines. The best years for steam were still ahead as its technology continued to advance. By this time, however, there was competition. The experiments of Leo Daft, Frank Sprague, and others led to the development of a successful electric locomotive. In 1895, in an effort to cut down air pollution, the B&O began operation of an electric locomotive to ferry trains in a tunnel under the city of Baltimore. After 1900, electrification took place on portions of the Pennsylvania and New Haven systems as well as on many suburban and elevated lines, but it was never a serious contender to the dominance of steam.

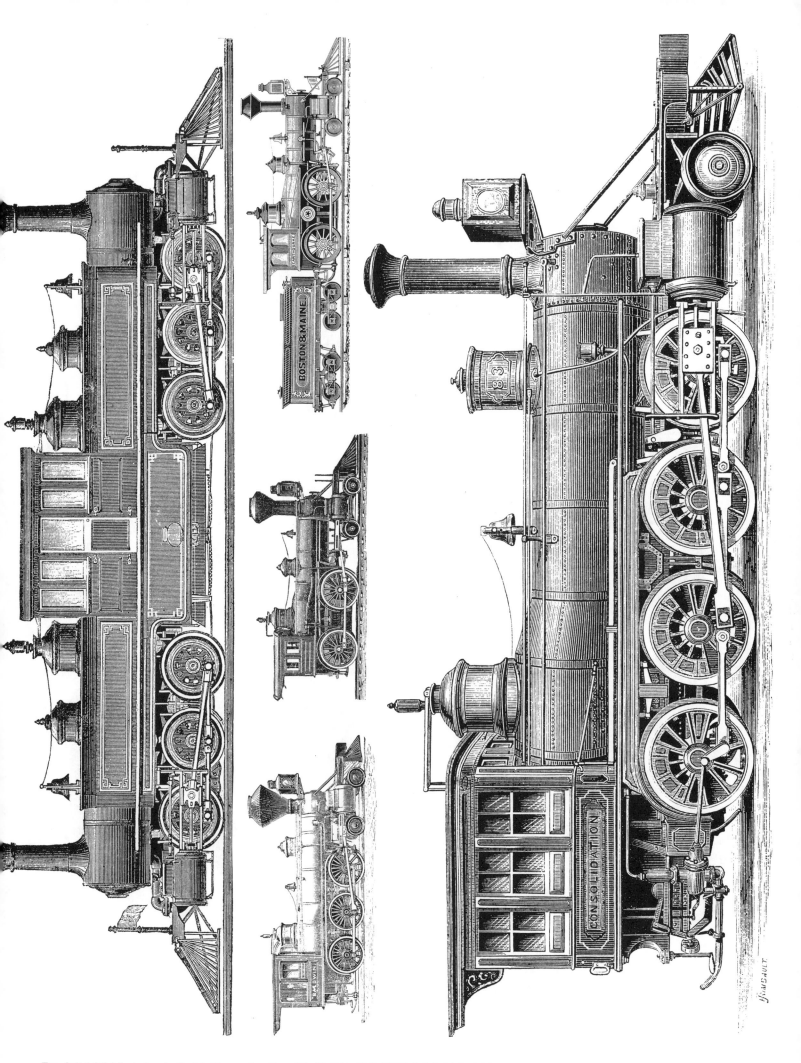

Top; 0-6+6-0 Fairlie designed articulated locomotive, Central Pacific R.R., 1869. Middle left; Baldwin 4-6-0 "Ten Wheeler" type, late 1860s. Middle center; Danforth 4-4-0 "American" type engine, c.1870s. Middle right; 4-4-0 passenger locomotive, Boston & Maine R.R., c.1870. Bottom; First 2-8-0 "Consolidation" type built by Baldwin for Lehigh Valley R.R., 1866.

59

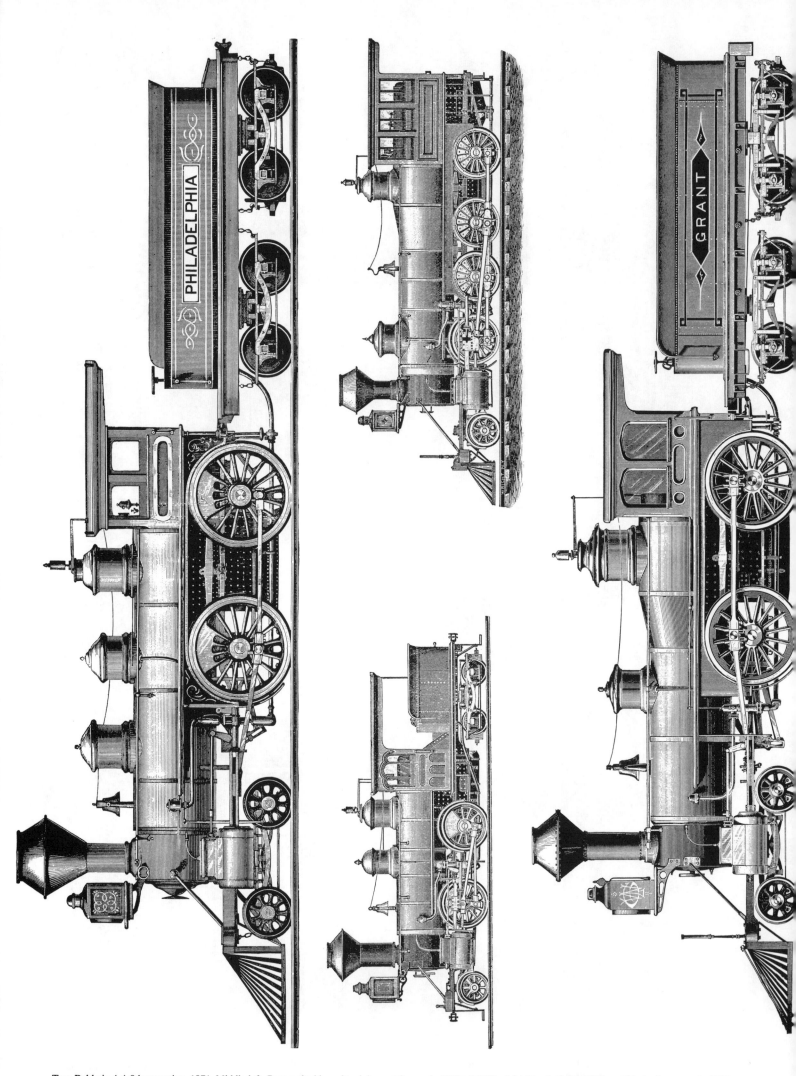

Top; Baldwin 4-4-0 locomotive, 1871. Middle left; Rogers double-end tank locomotive, early 1870s. Middle right; Danforth 2-8-0 "Consolidation" type, early 1870s. Bottom; Grant 4-4-0 locomotive, 1873.

Top; Forney locomotive with upright boiler for light traffic/frequent service use, 1872. Middle; Double-truck narrow gauge locomotive, Mason Machine Works, 1871. Bottom; Baldwin 2-6-0 "Mogul" type freight locomotive, 1872.

Classic 4-4-0 "American" type locomotives: Top; built by Mason Machine Works, c. 1874. Middle; probably from Camden & Amboy R.R., c. 1871. Bottom; built by the Hinkley Co., c. 1874.

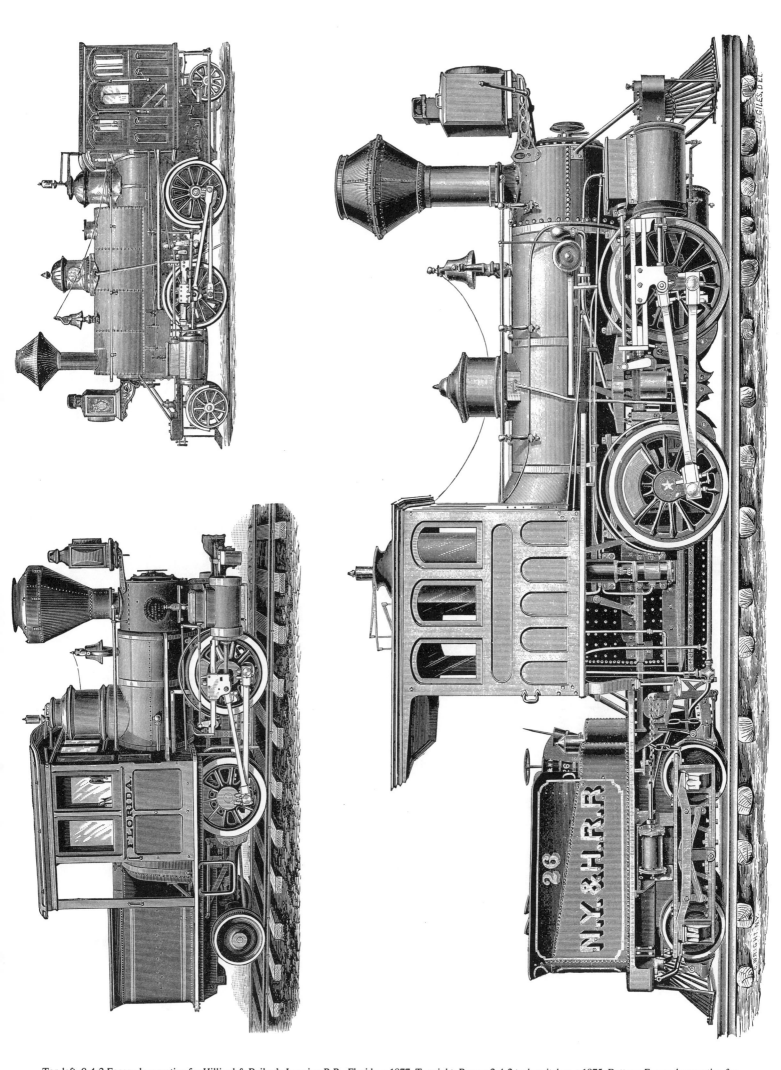

Top left; 0-4-2 Forney locomotive for Hilliard & Bailey's Logging R.R., Florida, c.1877. Top right; Rogers 2-4-2 tank switcher, c.1875. Bottom; Forney locomotive for suburban traffic, New York & Harlem R.R., 1876.

Top; Narrow gauge 0-4-4 Forney locomotive for Billerica & Bedford R.R., Massachusetts, 1877. Bottom; Baldwin 0-4-0 tank engine for The New York Elevated R.R., 1878.

Top; Baldwin 0-4-4 Forney locomotive for the New York Elevated R.R., 1878. Bottom; "Dummy" locomotive for the Metropolitan Elevated Railway, 1878.

Top; Manchester 2-6-0 "Mogul" type freight engine, 1879. Middle left; 0-6-0 tank switcher, c.1875. Middle right; Portland 4-4-0 passenger locomotive, c.1878. Bottom; Baldwin 2-8-0 tank locomotive, 1879.

Top; 0-4-4 Forney locomotive, Indianapolis & Evansville Rwy., 1880. Bottom; 2-6-6 narrow gauge double-truck tank locomotive, Denver, South Park & Pacific R.R., 1880.

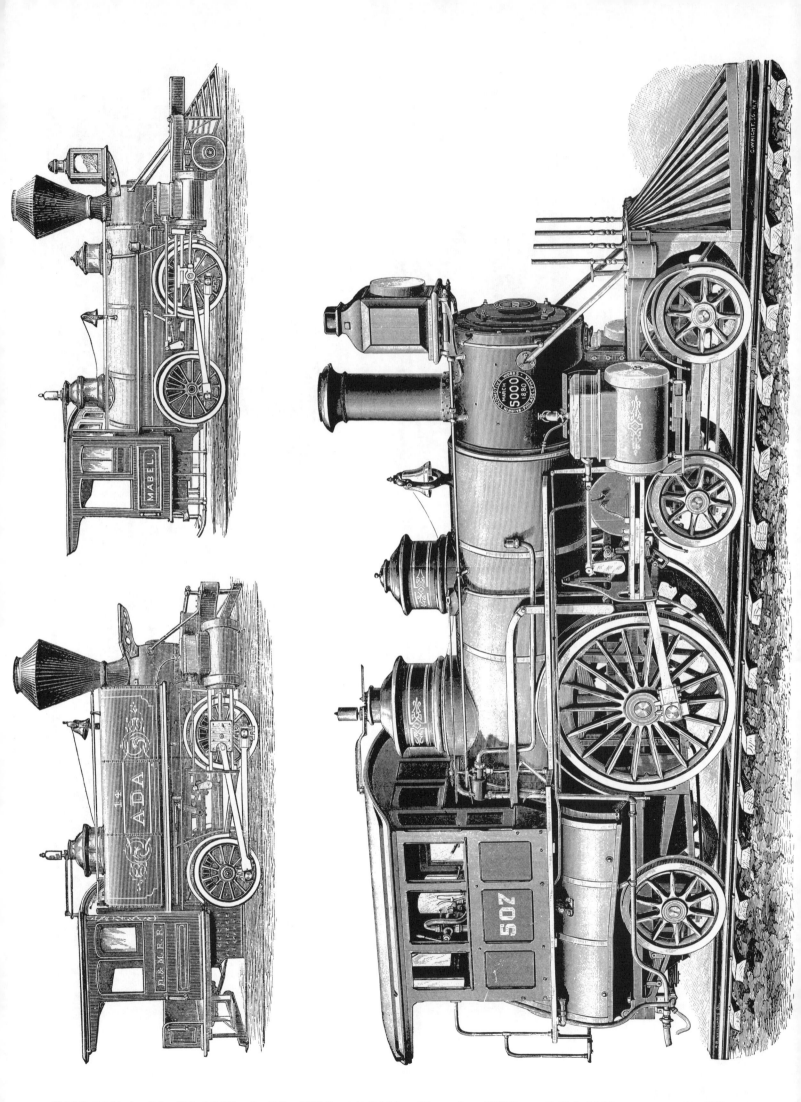

Top left; 0-4-0 tank switcher, Detroit & Milwaukee R.R., c.1875. Top right; 2-4-0 "pony" locomotive, c.1880. Bottom; Baldwin 4-2-2 fast passenger engine, 1880.

Top; Baldwin Locomotive Works, Philadelphia, c.1875. Bottom; The "Fontaine" locomotive, Grant Locomotive Works, 1881. This experimental engine, designed by Eugene Fontaine of Detroit, was sold to a Canadian railway.

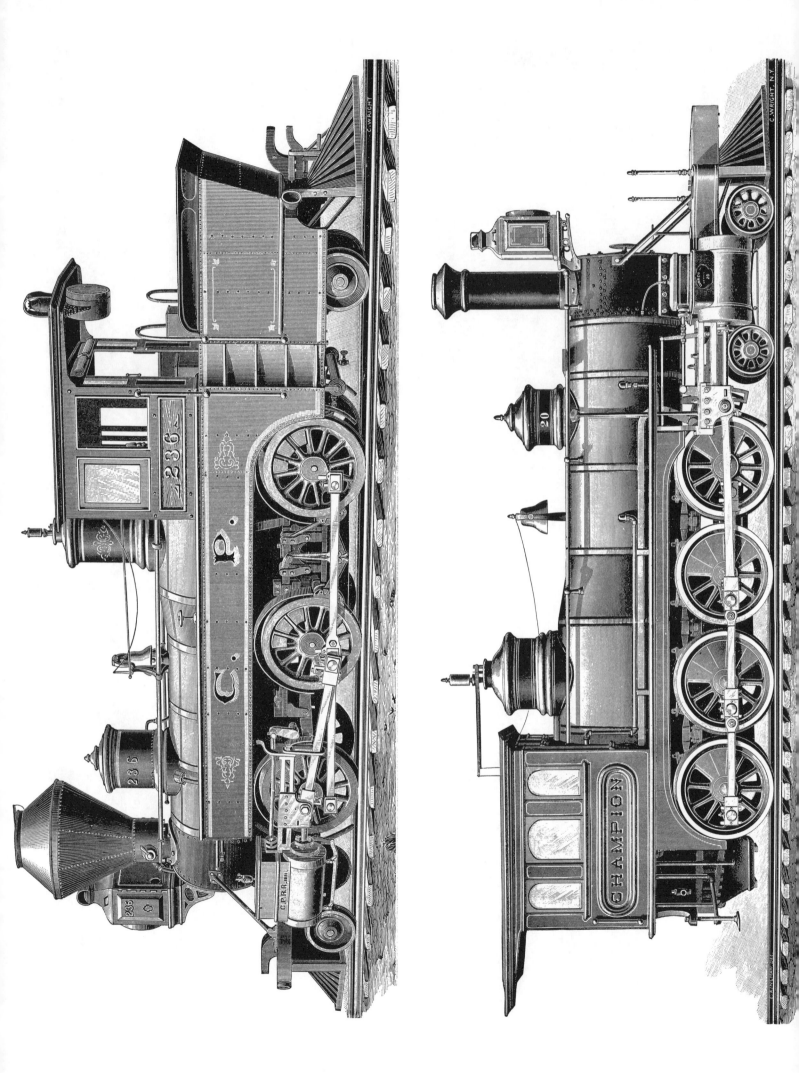

Top; Tank engine for suburban traffic, Central Pacific R.R., 1882. Bottom; 4-8-0 "Twelve Wheeler" type, Lehigh Valley R.R., 1882.

Top; Rogers 4-6-0 "Ten Wheeler" type freight engine, Southern Pacific of New Mexico R.R., early 1880s. Bottom; 4-4-0 "American" type, New York, New Haven & Hartford R.R., 1882.

71

Top; Dickson 0-4-2 tank switcher, 1885. Middle; Dickson 0-4-4 Forney tank locomotive, 1885. Bottom; Dickson 2-6-0 coupled switcher, 1885.

Top; Locomotive for "pole" roads, Tanner & Delaney Engine Co., 1886. Middle; Car for "pole" road use [usually for carrying logs]. Bottom; Porter mining locomotive, c.1886.

Top left; Baldwin 2-4-0 "pony" locomotive for suburban traffic, 1880s. Top right; Rogers 0-4-4 Forney tank locomotive, 1880s. Middle right; Porter 0-4-2 engine, c.1889. Bottom; Rogers 0-6-0 switcher, c.1888. The M & T marking on the tender probably indicates that it was either the Mississippi & Tennessee R.R. or the Monterey & Tampico Ry. of Mexico.

Top left; 2-6-0 "Mogul" type locomotive, Maine Central R.R., c.1889. Top right; 2-8-0 "Consolidation" type, Pennsylvania R.R., c.1889. Middle; 4-4-0 passenger engine, P. R.R., c.1889. Bottom; 4-6-0 "Ten Wheeler" type, fast passenger locomotive, Maine Central R.R., c.1890.

Locomotive for cog railroad, Manitou & Pike's Peak R.R., Colorado, 1891.

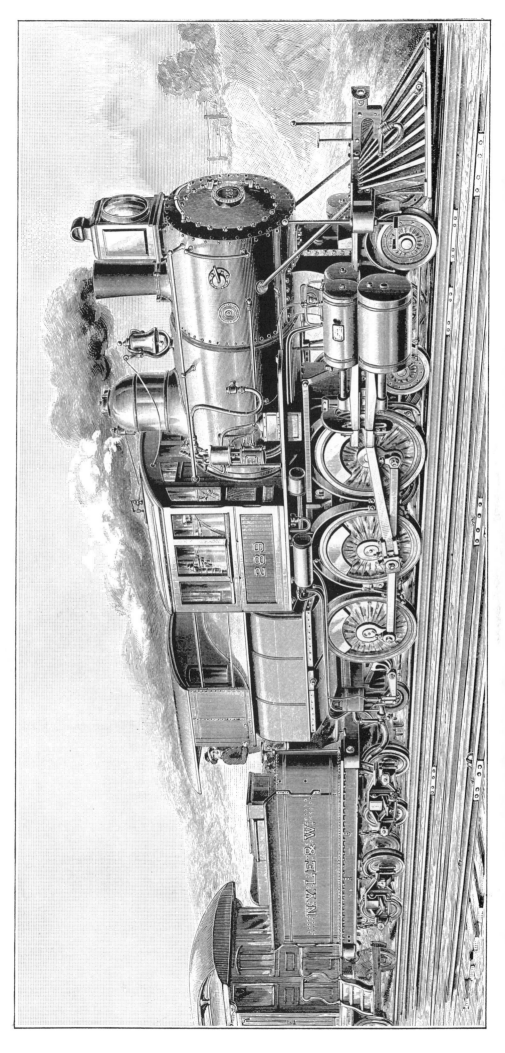

Top left; Rogers 4-6-0 "Ten Wheeler" type locomotive, Charleston & Savannah Rwy., 1893. Top right; Baldwin 0-6-0 switcher, c.1889. Middle right; Baldwin 2-10-0 Decapod engine, 1886. Bottom; 4-6-0 "Ten Wheeler" type locomotive with Wootten firebox; New York, Lake Erie & Western R.R., c.1891.

Top; 4-4-0 compound engine built by Rhode Island Locomotive Works, New York, New Haven & Hartford R.R., 1893. Bottom; Baldwin 0-10-0 tank locomotive, with Wootten firebox, for use in St. Clair Tunnel on U.S.-Canada border, 1891.

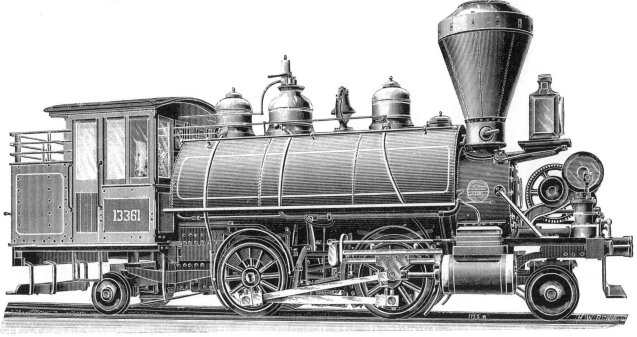

Locomotives exhibited at the Columbian Exposition, Chicago, in 1893: Top; Baldwin 0-4-0 tank switcher. Middle left; Porter 0-4-0 tank switcher. Middle right; Porter 0-4-2 logging engine. Bottom; Baldwin 2-4-2 logging locomotive.

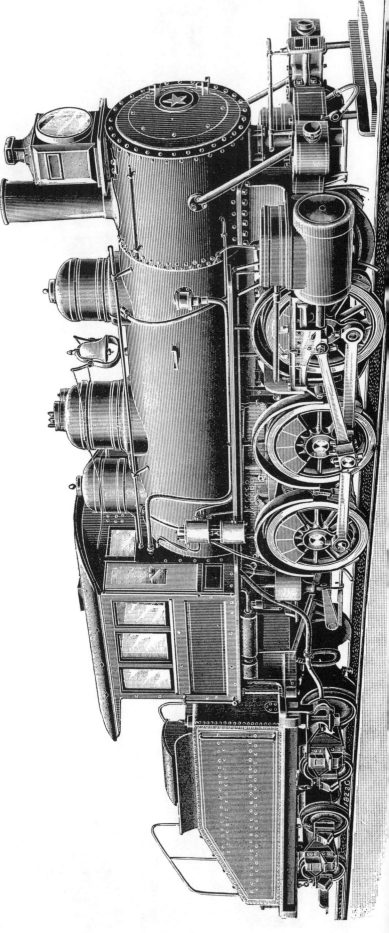

Locomotives exhibited at the Columbian Exposition in 1893: Top; Brooks 0-6-0 switcher, Great Northern R.R. Bottom; Schenectady Locomotive Works 0-6-0 switcher.

4-4-0 "American" type passenger locomotives exhibited at the Columbian Exposition in 1893: Top; Baldwin engine, Baltimore & Ohio R.R. Middle; Baldwin locomotive. Bottom; Rogers engine, Chicago, Burlington & Quincy R.R.

4-4-0 "American" type passenger locomotives exhibited at the Columbian Exposition in 1893: Top; Baldwin locomotive, Central Railroad of New Jersey. Middle; Famous New York Central engine No. 999. Bottom; Brooks locomotive, Cincinnati, Hamilton & Dayton R.R.

4-4-0 "American" type passenger locomotives exhibited at the Columbian Exposition in 1893: Top; Baldwin engine, Baltimore & Ohio R.R. Middle; Baldwin locomotive, B. & O. R.R. Bottom; Engine of Lake Shore & Michigan Southern R.R.

Locomotives exhibited at the Columbian Exposition in 1893: Top; Baldwin 4-4-0 compound passenger or freight locomotive. Upper middle; Baldwin 2-4-2 "Columbia" type locomotive. Lower middle; Baldwin 2-4-2 "Columbia" type compound express engine with Wootten firebox, Philadelphia & Reading R.R. Bottom; Porter 2-6-0 "Mogul" type.

Locomotives exhibited at the Columbian Exposition in 1893: Top; Brooks 2-6-6 tank locomotive for suburban traffic, Chicago & Northern Pacific R.R. Middle; Baldwin 2-6-0 "Mogul" type. Bottom; Brooks 2-6-0 "Mogul" type, Great Northern R.R.

4-6-0 "Ten Wheeler" type locomotives exhibited at the Columbian Exposition in 1893: Top; Brooks passenger engine, Great Northern R.R. Middle; Baldwin locomotive, Baltimore & Ohio R.R. Bottom; Brooks 2-cylinder compound freight locomotive, Lake Shore & Michigan Southern R.R.

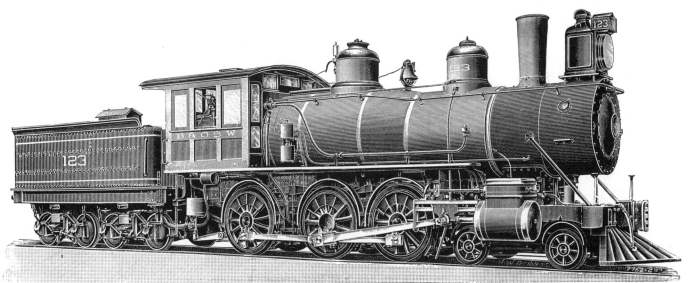

4-6-0 "Ten Wheeler" type locomotives exhibited at the Columbian Exposition in 1893: Top; Brooks passenger locomotive, Lake Shore & Michigan Southern R.R.
Middle; Baldwin freight locomotive. Bottom; Schenectady passenger engine, Chicago & North Western R.R.

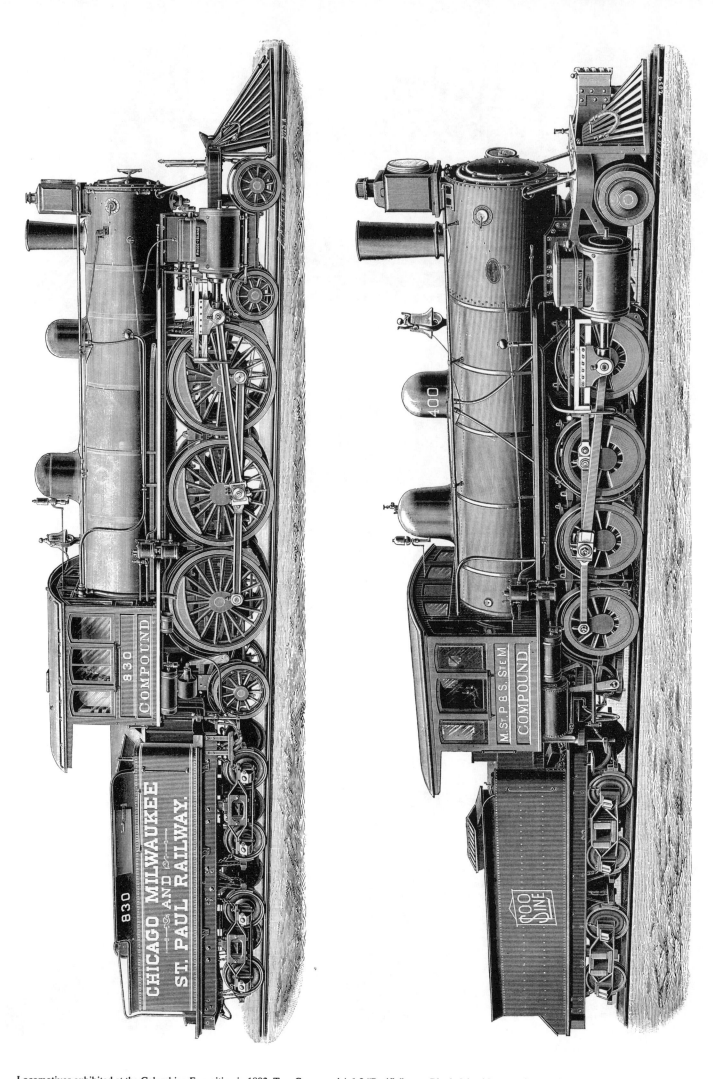

Locomotives exhibited at the Columbian Exposition in 1893: Top; Compound 4-6-2 "Pacific" type, Rhode Island Locomotive Works. Bottom; Rhode Island compound 2-8-0 "Consolidation" type, Minneapolis, St. Paul & Sault Ste. Marie R.R.

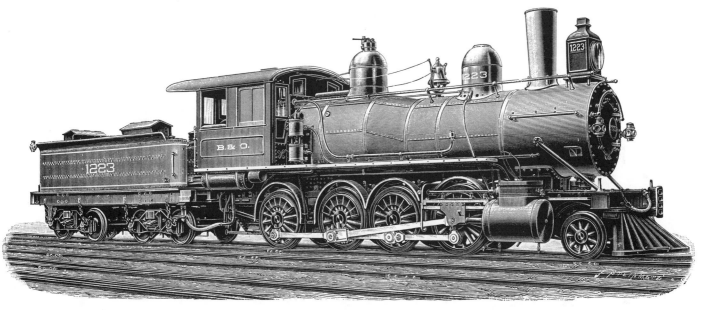

2-8-0 "Consolidation" type freight locomotives exhibited at the Columbian Exposition in 1893: Top; Baldwin engine, Norfolk & Western R.R. Middle; Baldwin locomotive, Baltimore & Ohio R.R. Bottom; Schenectady engine, Mohawk & Malone R.R.

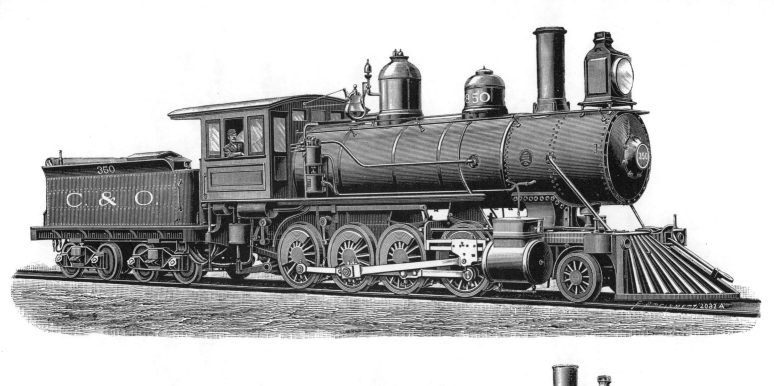

2-8-0 "Consolidation" type freight locomotives exhibited at the Columbian Exposition in 1893: Top; Richmond locomotive, Chesapeake & Ohio R.R. Middle; Rogers engine, Illinois Central R.R. Bottom; Brooks compound locomotive, Great Northern R.R.

Locomotives exhibited at the Columbian Exposition in 1893: Top; Schenectady 4-8-0 "Twelve Wheeler" type, Duluth & Iron Range R.R. Middle; Brooks 4-8-0 "Twelve Wheeler" type, Great Northern R.R. Bottom; Baldwin 2-10-0 "Decapod" type with Wootten firebox, New York, Lake Erie & Western R.R.

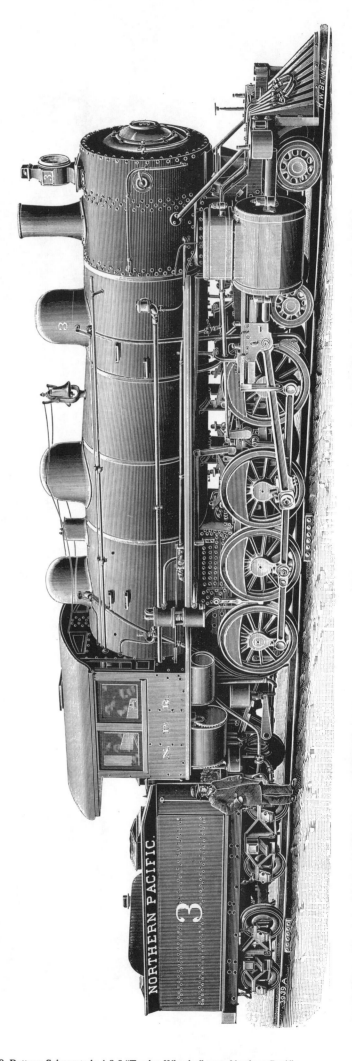

Top; Brooks 4-6-0 "Ten Wheeler" passenger engine, Buffalo, Rochester & Pittsburgh Ry., 1899. Bottom; Schenectady 4-8-0 "Twelve Wheeler" type, Northern Pacific R.R., 1897.

The new Baltimore & Ohio electric locomotive pulling passenger train in tunnel under Baltimore, 1896.

Following the Civil War the United States enjoyed an economic expansion. With the of vast amounts of foreign capital, railroads built ever denser networks in the Northeast and Midwest, and more trunk lines were formed. Over a longer period railroads in the South were restored and expanded. However, it was the spread of railroad lines into the West that now captured the public imagination. The biggest news story of the time was the progress of the transcontinental line as the Union Pacific crossed Nebraska up the Platte River, and the Central Pacific labored to get over the Sierra Nevada range. On May 10, 1869, when the two lines joined for the golden-spike ceremony at Promontory Point, Utah, near the Great Salt Lake, the entire nation cheered.

Even as early as the 1830s there had been a few visionary individuals who foresaw the possibility of a railroad to the West Coast. In the 1840s, Asa Whitney, a businessman who had traveled to China, tried to interest Congress in the idea. Following the discovery of gold in California in 1848 and that state's entry into the Union in 1850, there seemed to be more practical reasons for such a rail line. Debate began, with various sections of the country pushing their own agendas. The South wanted a route that went through Texas to southern California. The far North wanted a route that began at Lake Superior. Most people in the East and Midwest preferred a more central route originating either in Chicago or St. Louis, but there was considerable argument there as well.

In March 1853 Congress passed a bill authorizing Jefferson Davis, the secretary of war, to send out army survey crews to determine the most practical route. Later that same year, James Gadsden persuaded Mexico to sell the U.S. an area that would eventually become part of southern Arizona and southeastern New Mexico. This new land provided an easy passage over the Continental Divide. The surveys were carried out and it appeared the southern route was the easiest to build. However, debate in Washington became ever more as the war approached, and no agreement could be reached.

There had been interest in California as well. Theodore Judah, who built the first railroad in the state from Sacramento to the gold country, became a strong promoter for the line. He attracted some important backers and went to Washington to lobby for its passage in 1859. Judah later died, having contracted yellow fever while crossing the Isthmus of Panama on one of his lobbying trips. However, his backers Leland Stanford, Charles Crocker, Mark Hopkins, and C. P. Huntington continued the effort and later became the chief officers of the Central Pacific.

In 1862 President Lincoln signed two pieces of legislation that would greatly affect the future of the West. The first of these was the Homestead Act, which allowed any party to file for 160 acres of public domain land. If that individual then occupied the land for five consecutive years he would become the owner. Later, Lincoln signed the Pacific Railroad Act. This authorized construction of the line over a central route, with the Union Pacific beginning in Nebraska and the Central Pacific starting in San Francisco, to later join one another. It gave each railroad a free right of way, with land for other rail facilities, and five alternate sections of land on each side of the track. Generous loans were furnished for each mile of construction based on the type of terrain. It was thought that the railroads could sell this land to settlers, thus creating a base for future revenues. In 1864 another bill was passed authorizing the Northern Pacific to build a railroad from Lake Superior to Puget Sound.

The Union Pacific began building from Omaha. Unfortunately, its chief officers were both inept and corrupt, and only when they hired General Grenville M. Dodge as chief construction engineer did things improve. The construction was difficult and time-consuming, using large crews of men and pack animals. Irish immigrant workers, many who had previously worked for the Erie or other lines, provided most of the labor. Conditions were often harsh, as the Indians were hostile and the winter weather bitterly cold. The workers themselves were a rather rough group, given to carousing and occasional violence. The construction activity was followed in the rear by prostitutes, liquor salesmen, gamblers, and other predatory individuals.

Despite having more difficult terrain to build through, the Central Pacific had other things in its favor. It took early steps to pacify the Indians, and soon discovered that Chinese immigrants made excellent workers: they were stable, practical, had better habits, and preferred tea to whiskey. The Central Pacific recruited as many Chinese as possible in California and then sent agents to China to recruit more.

As the two railroads made more progress they began to race one another, with the Central Pacific finally constructing ten miles of track in a single day. At last the two met in an elaborate ceremony when the presidents of both railroads and other officials and dignitaries arrived. A final golden spike was driven in and a locomotive from each line steamed up to face the other. The news was quickly telegraphed to the eager nation: a new era had been born.

In 1869 the Santa Fe Railroad began laying rails westward from Topeka, Kansas, closely following the Santa Fe Trail; by 1880 it reached Santa Fe. At the same time construction crews were laying Southern Pacific track across the desert from Los Angeles. They met at Deming, New Mexico, in 1881, becoming the second completed transcontinental line. It wasn't until 1883 that the two lines of the Northern Pacific met at Gold Creek, Montana, to become the third completed line. In 1893 the Great Northern Railroad celebrated completion of its own northern route, having an iron-spike ceremony in a Cascade snowstorm.

Other lines expanded in the West. The Kansas Pacific Railroad crossed through Kansas in the late 1860s, drawing herds of Texas cattle to Abilene for shipment to Chicago. It reached Denver in 1871. The Denver & Rio Grande Western, losing Raton Pass in a confrontation with the Santa Fe, was left with a difficult route. It built south from Denver to Pueblo and then west through Royal Gorge, through Tennessee Pass, into the Colorado River Valley and on to Salt Lake City. There it connected with the Western Pacific, which reached through Nevada to Oakland.

Other lines were also built in the West. As an influx of settlers came to the region, railroads extended out branches in many directions, forming an ever stronger network. Railroad competition was cutthroat at times, and often those officials who controlled the lines became enormously wealthy at the expense of their investors, the government, and those whom the railroads served. Despite this, however, a great work had been performed, allowing for the settlement of the West and its economic and political integration into the rest of the country.

Slaughter of buffalo on the Kansas Pacific R.R., 1867.

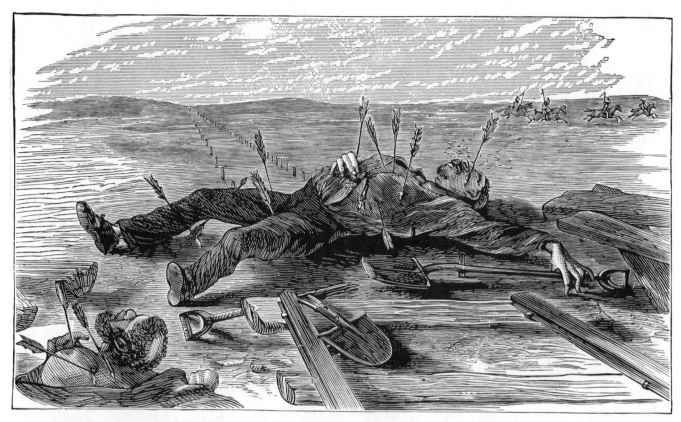

Top; Irish construction workers killed by Indians, Union Pacific R.R. c.1869. Bottom; Indians viewing a passing train, c.1869.

Top; Union Pacific train attacked by Indians east of Cheyenne, Wyo., 1870. Bottom; Completion of the Pacific Railroad: special train of the Central Pacific pulled by the locomotive, "Jupiter," Promontory Point, Utah, May 10, 1869.

Top; Passenger train passing the Pallisades, Ten-Mile Canyon, Nev., Central Pacific R.R., c.1870. Bottom; Completion of the Pacific Railroad: locomotives of the Central Pacific and Union Pacific meet and the engineers shake hands, May 10, 1869.

Left; Construction of snow sheds on Central Pacific R.R., c.1869. Right; Snow sheds covered by snow, c.1870.

Activity at station on the Great Plains, Union Pacific R.R., 1869.

Top; Deer race ahead of Union Pacific train west of Omaha, Nebr., 1870. Bottom; "The First Train," 1869.

Top; Laying track on the Pacific Railway. Bottom; The ferry "Solano," which began service across the Carquinez Straits in Dec. 1879, carried complete trains between Benicia and Port Acosta, Calif. This service reduced travel time on the Central Pacific line between Sacramento and San Francisco to four hours.

Railroad building on the Great Plains, Northern Pacific R.R., 1875.

Union Pacific R.R. scenes in Nebraska, 1877: Top; East and west bound trains pass each other near Fremont. Middle; Departure of an east bound train, Schuyler Station. Bottom; Arrival at the town of Columbus.

Narrow gauge railroad scenes in Colorado in the early 1880s. Top; Trains ascending Marshall Pass, elevation 10,846 ft., Denver & Rio Grande R.R. Bottom; View of Denver, South Park & Pacific R.R. line along the South Platte River southwest of Denver.

Narrow gauge line through Royal Gorge, Colo., Denver & Rio Grande R.R., c. early 1880s.

Completion of the Northern Pacific Railroad: driving the last spike at the point of junction between the eastern and western sections, sixty miles west of Helena, Mont., Sept. 8, 1883.

A herd of antelope delaying a Denver & Rio Grande Western train, near Green River, Utah, 1884.

5 · MOVING PASSENGERS

In the general expansion of the railroads following the end of the war, passenger service played its role. Service was provided to new areas and increased in the places where business warranted it. Trains became faster, and new developments in the design of passenger cars gave rail travel an unprecedented new look of luxury, convenience, and comfort. In 1865, George M. Pullman introduced his new sleeping car, the *Pioneer,* just in time to have it carry President Lincoln's body, after his assassination, on its funeral journey. Though sleeping cars were not new, this one pioneered a number of innovations that would help to revolutionize passenger travel in the years to come. The history of sleeping cars goes back to a railroad surveyor, R. R. Morgan, who displayed a design for such a car at Faneuil Hall, Boston, in 1829. In 1836 the Cumberland Valley Railroad built the first sleeper, operating it between Philadelphia and Baltimore. Soon other railroads began building their own versions, and by the year 1848 the Griffin-Atlanta Railroad in Georgia was using cars having triple-decker sleeping berths. Later, Theodore T. Woodruff developed an idea for a hinged, pull-out berth, located above the car windows, and secured a patent in 1856.

Pullman became interested in the design of sleepers in 1858, after his first ride on one. Beginning in 1859, he tested a number of his ideas on the Chicago & Alton Railroad. Shortly after this, however, he left for Colorado and made a small fortune selling supplies to miners. Returning to Chicago in 1864, he organized the Pullman Palace Car Company and introduced the *Pioneer* the following year. Soon his cars were operating on a number of railroads and quickly became popular. In 1867 Pullman introduced the hotel car, a combination sleeper and dining car. In 1868, the *Delmonico,* his first all-dining car, began operation on the Chicago & Alton line. Pullman's cars, making their appearance just before the completion of the Pacific Railroad, could not have come at a more timely moment.

The March 20, 1875, issue of the *Illustrated London News* briefly describes a train of Pullman cars:

The train consists of a variety of cars—the drawing room sleeping car, which can be quickly converted into a day car, without leaving any evidence of the purpose for which it has been used at night; the parlour car, for short lines and day travel only; and the hotel car, which is the same as the drawing room sleeping car, but also contains kitchen and buffet, with adjustable tables, to accommodate a full complement of passengers for long journeys and excursion parties. The internal decorations and fittings are magnificent. The woodwork is of walnut, with ornamentation of gold and ebony, silver-gilt mountings, or medallions in bronze. Above are fresco ceilings, from which descend elegantly designed lamps, which give forth a brilliant flame. Handsome carpets cover the floors; the seats are of cushioned velvet; highly polished mirrors in gilt frames decorate the walls, those at the end giving an appearance of great length to the car. In fact, so far as convenience, comfort, and luxury are concerned, Pullman's Palace Cars are, to all intents and

purposes, first class hotels, of one story, mounted on wheels. All this provision for the solace and gratification of travelers is needed to beguile their weary long journey from New York to San Francisco, a distance of three thousand miles, which occupies six days, moving on day and night.

Pullman's cars began operation in England in 1874 and were later exported elsewhere. In addition to providing his cars for use by railroads, he supplied the porters and other staff as well, giving them special job training. Pullman also built luxury cars for the private use of the wealthy. These cars could be coupled onto trains and taken to any location. In 1886 he introduced the Vestibuled Limited Train, a train composed of handsomely designed cars having flexible vestibule passageways connecting them. This allowed a much safer and easier passage when moving between cars.

Pullman did have a number of competitors, the most prominent of whom was Webster Wagner. Wagner began building and operating Woodruff-designed sleepers for the New York Central in 1858. In 1866, when Cornelius Vanderbilt gained control of the railroads using Wagner's cars, the company was forced to reorganize under terms imposed by the Commodore. First called the New York Central Sleeping Car Company, it was later changed to the Wagner Palace Car Company. Wagner was burned up in one of his own cars in a train wreck at Spuyten Duyvil, New York, on January 13, 1882. The company continued in operation for a while under the Vanderbilts but was purchased by Pullman in 1900.

While the luxury cars of Pullman, Wagner, and others captured the attention of the media, the great majority of travelers made their journeys by the less expensive chair cars, and usually on trains other than fast expresses or limiteds. Before the Civil War, railroads had begun providing an even lower grade of transportation for poor European immigrants who could afford no better. After the war, with ever greater numbers of arrivals, this traffic increased considerably. The uncomfortable passenger cars typically used for this purpose were either old or converted from boxcars. They had only rudimentary seats and toilets and poor ventilation. They were either coupled to regular trains or made up into special immigrant trains. These were given the lowest priority and were slow in reaching their destinations.

In the early years of railroads, food and drink were either carried on by the traveler or purchased from local people at train stops. Soon stations and trackside restaurants began offering food and refreshment, but this was usually of poor quality. The first dining cars were built by the B&O line in 1848 and offered simple meals. Later, after the introduction of Pullman's dining cars, railroad food service reached a much higher level for those who could afford it, offering a wider range of selections and more elegant decor. However, trains on many lines continued to make meal stops. The famous Harvey House restaurant was first introduced in 1876 on the Santa Fe line in Topeka, Kansas, and later became a successful chain. On most railroads food service continued to improve to the end of the century.

"The Rush for the Country," 1868.

Top; Typical passenger train, mid-1860s. Bottom; A train waiting for departure, Stratford, Conn., 1867.

"Home for the Holidays," 1869.

Top; Dining car on the Pacific Railroad, 1869. Bottom; "Constructing Railroad Ties," a scene on the Erie Limited, 1872.

Dining car on the Pacific Railroad, c.1872.

Top; Refreshment stop in North Carolina for a Florida bound train. Bottom; A train of German immigrants departing Chicago for Colorado; Chicago & St. Louis R.R., 1870.

A Sunday religious gathering on a Union Pacific train, 1875.

Interior of a Pullman Parlor Car on the Pennsylvania R.R., between New York and Philadelphia, 1876: Left; The smoking saloon. Right; The parlor.

Car interior of a west bound immigrant train, 1881.

Car interior on the "legislative train," from Albany to New York; New York Central R.R., 1882.

Top; Departure from Communipaw of New York National Guardsmen for Mardi Gras, 1881. Bottom; Departure at Grand Central Station in New York of publisher Frank Leslie and party for a transcontinental journey, 1877.

Top; Chinese passengers disembarking at Erie terminal in Jersey City, N.J., for ferry trip to New York, 1880. Bottom; Erie passenger trains at Hornellsville, N.Y., a division point on the line, c.1884.

Passenger trains on the scenic Pennsylvania R.R. Top; Horse-Shoe Curve, near Kittanning Point, Pa. Bottom; Jack's Narrows, viewed from Mapleton, Pa.

Customs officer at Canadian border checking baggage on a night train, Rouse's Point, N.Y., Delaware & Hudson R.R., 1883.

"All Aboard!"—Scene in the lunch room of a railroad station, 1886.

Top; "In the Waiting Room of a Country Station," 1888. Bottom; "The Trials of a Baggage Master," 1888.

The new "Ghost" express train between New York and Boston; New York, New Haven & Hartford R.R., 1891.

Suburban passenger trains: Top; Trains at a junction in Chicago, c.1896. Middle; Suburban Rapid Transit crossing on the Harlem River, 1885 [in left foreground are New York, New Haven & Hartford R.R. yards]. Bottom; Trains beneath a viaduct at the Philadelphia & Reading R.R. terminal, Philadelphia, 1891.

Rock Island passenger train operating between Chicago and Denver, c.1895.

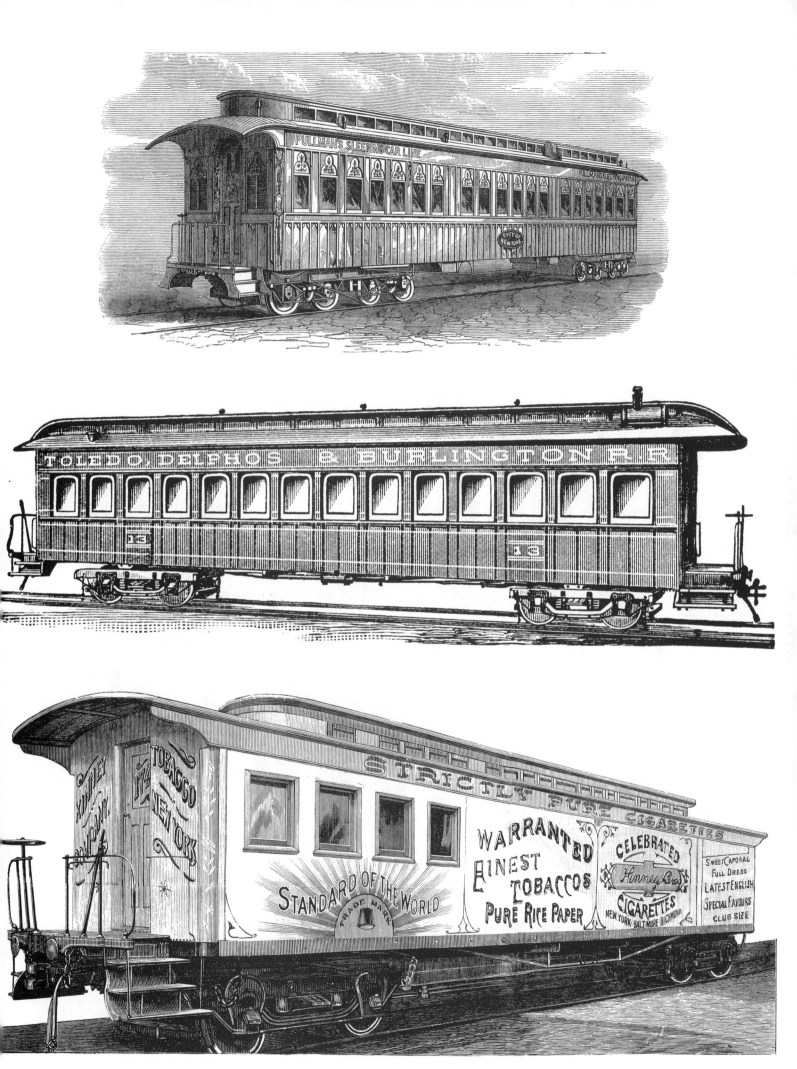

Top; Pullman sleeping car, 1869. Middle; Passenger car, c.1869. Bottom; Company owned car, Kinney Tobacco Co., 1887.

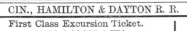

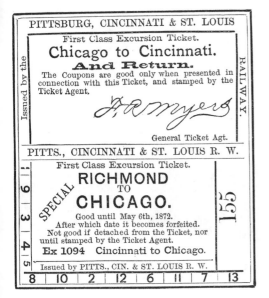

Top; *Scientific American* illustration of an inventor's proposed observatory sleeping car, c.1887. Left middle and left bottom; railroad tickets, 1872. Right bottom; End of coach showing improved car step, 1879.

Top; Combination baggage and passenger car, c.1879. Bottom; Interior of Kellogg's improved sleeping car, 1887.

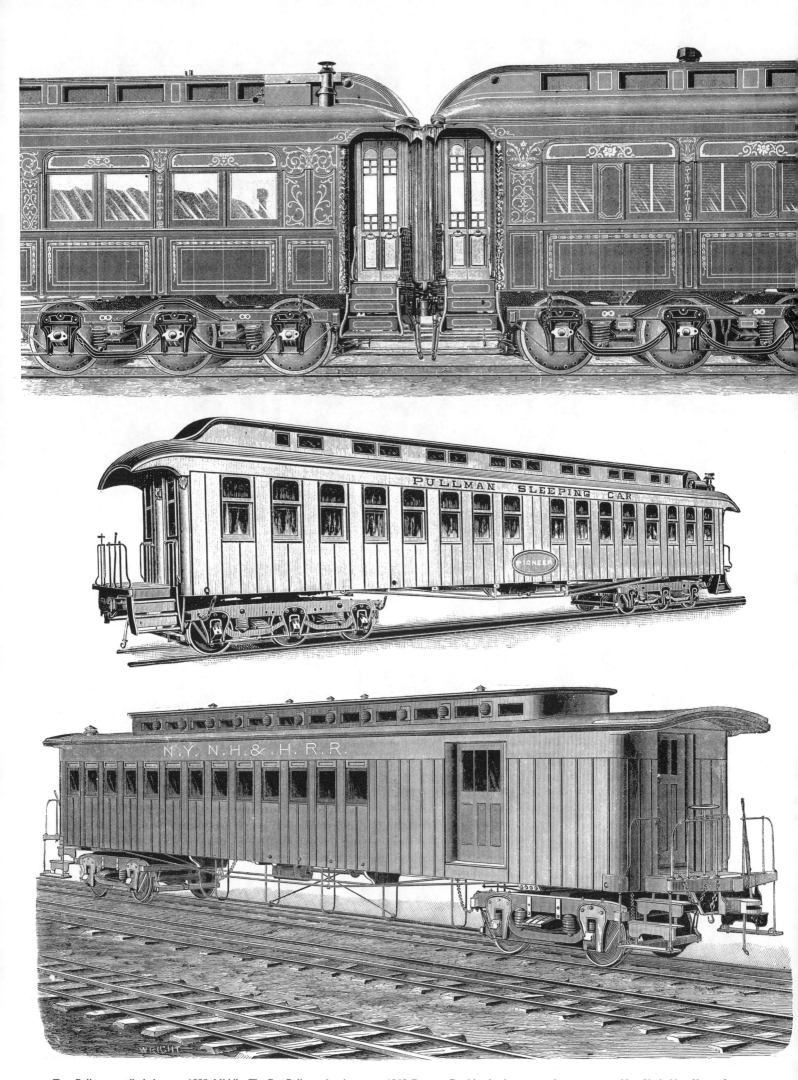

Top; Pullman vestibuled cars, c.1888. Middle; The first Pullman sleeping car, c. 1865. Bottom; Combination baggage and passenger car, New York, New Haven & Hartford R.R., 1885.

6·PASSENGER STATIONS AND TERMINALS

As lines expanded and traffic increased following the Civil War, station facilities, especially in the areas of more established commerce, were improved. Throughout America, in city and town alike, the train station provided a vital connecting link with the rest of the nation and the world. In small towns, especially, depots played an important role, bringing relief from an otherwise isolated and often monotonous existence. The arrival of a train became a daily social ritual for the community, bringing excitement and activity, news from the outside world, and a chance to encounter people—friends and strangers, travelers and the merely curious. Here one might receive letters or newspapers, exchange gossip, pick up an express shipment, send a telegram, meet an attractive member of the opposite sex, observe the general commotion, admire the locomotive and cars, or board the train. In time hotels, livery stables, cafes, and other establishments often built up around stations, providing the nucleus for a larger community. Small-town stations might typically have a waiting room, a ticket and telegraph office, a baggage room, and separate restrooms for men and women. In keeping with the spirit of the age, ornamental devices such as clock towers, bay windows, stained glass, dormer roofs, turrets, elaborate chimneys, finials, gables, and gingerbread were employed by architects to make stations look more attractive and stylish. This rather inclusive style became known as "railway gothic." Beginning about 1880, some lines also adopted the practice of having several standardized sets of designs for their stations; these were based upon serving communities of different sizes.

In the major cities, a few railway magnates, like Cornelius Vanderbilt, spared no expense in hiring some of America's finest architects to build a number of truly monumental stations. Vanderbilt's Grand Central Depot, begun in 1869, and located at 42nd Street and Fourth Avenue in Manhattan, was situated upon what had previously been a small stop on his New York and Harlem line that had its terminal at 26th Street. The new station, completed in 1871, was done in a renaissance style and had a French mansard roof. The New Haven, Harlem, and New York Central & Hudson River lines all had their facilities inside. In the rear of the station a beautiful arched train shed of cast iron and glass protected both trains and passengers from any bad weather. The northbound tracks leading away from the station were originally at ground level, however, many accidents occurred with crossing traffic. This led to an open cut being made where railroad traffic ran beneath that of street-level traffic.

Because of Manhattan's unique situation as a densely populated island, railroads had difficulty gaining access into it.

Lines like the Erie, Pennsylvania, and Lackawanna that came in from the west had terminals on the New Jersey side of the Hudson River, and had to ferry their passengers to and from Manhattan. Only after the turn of the century did a subway open that connected the New Jersey terminals with stations in Manhattan. A little later, the Pennsylvania Railroad tunneled into the city.

Boston's Park Square Station, begun in 1872 for the Boston & Providence Railroad and built in the English gothic style, was not such an immense structure, but it pioneered what was to become a greater emphasis on human comfort. Besides having a nice clock tower, it contained a reading room, a billiard room, and a barbershop. Another of the great terminals was the Pennsylvania Railroad Broad Street Station in Philadelphia. Opening December 5, 1881, it was located across the street from City Hall, and in addition to serving the public, it housed the central offices of the railroad. It originally had eight tracks leading into it, compared with twelve in New York's Grand Central Depot, but more were added later. Chicago's Grand Central Station, built in 1890 by the Baltimore & Ohio Railroad, had stained-glass windows, marble floors, a huge fireplace, various other ornamented features, and an immigrants' room. The Union Station in St. Louis, largest in the country when it opened in 1894, was a curious American blending of the Romanesque and the *belle époque.* South Boston Station, terminus for the Old Colony, Boston & Albany, and New Haven lines, opened its doors in 1899. Serving 50 million passengers in 1900, it was the world's largest railway station until 1910.

In his book, *Encyclopedia of North American Railroading,* Freeman Hubbard describes five types of stations:

1) Through station, built beside tracks or under them in such a way that trains pass through it directly in either direction, a setup which eliminates a lot of switching...
2) Way station, usually built to straddle the tracks, often consisting of buildings on both sides of the tracks and connected by a tunnel or an overpass...
3) Stub station, one in which the tracks stop abruptly, so that trains must head in, back in, or depart in reverse...
4) Loop station, one having an oval-shaped track connecting with the mainline so that trains proceeding via the loop head directly into their tracks beside the depot platform...
5) Terminal station, built at the end of a railroad line, usually at the end of the mainline.

Grand Central Station, 42nd St. and 4th Ave., New York City, 1872.

Grand Central Station, interior of train shed, c.1872.

135

Sinking the tracks of the New York & Harlem R.R. north of Grand Central Station, view from 126th St. and 4th Ave. looking south. This picture of 1873 illustrates the way it was shortly to look.

New York, Lake Erie & Western R.R. depot, at foot of Chambers St., New York, 1884. From here passengers would be ferried across the Hudson to terminal at Jersey City, N.J.

Erie terminal and docks, Jersey City, N.J., 1884.

Terminal of the North Hudson County R.R., Weehawken, N.J., opposite New York, 1891. Giant elevator carried passengers between the railroad facility and the ferry dock below. Top; View from a distance. Bottom; View from the dock.

Top; Views of Pennsylvania R.R. terminal and ferry docks, Jersey City, N.J., 1891. Bottom; Docks at terminus of the Central Pacific R.R., Oakland, Calif., 1871.

Pennsylvania R.R. Station, Broad St., Philadelphia, c. early 1880s.

Rear view of Pennsylvania R.R. Station, Broad St., after remodeling and enlarging, 1892.

Pennsylvania R.R. Centennial Depot, Philadelphia, 1876.

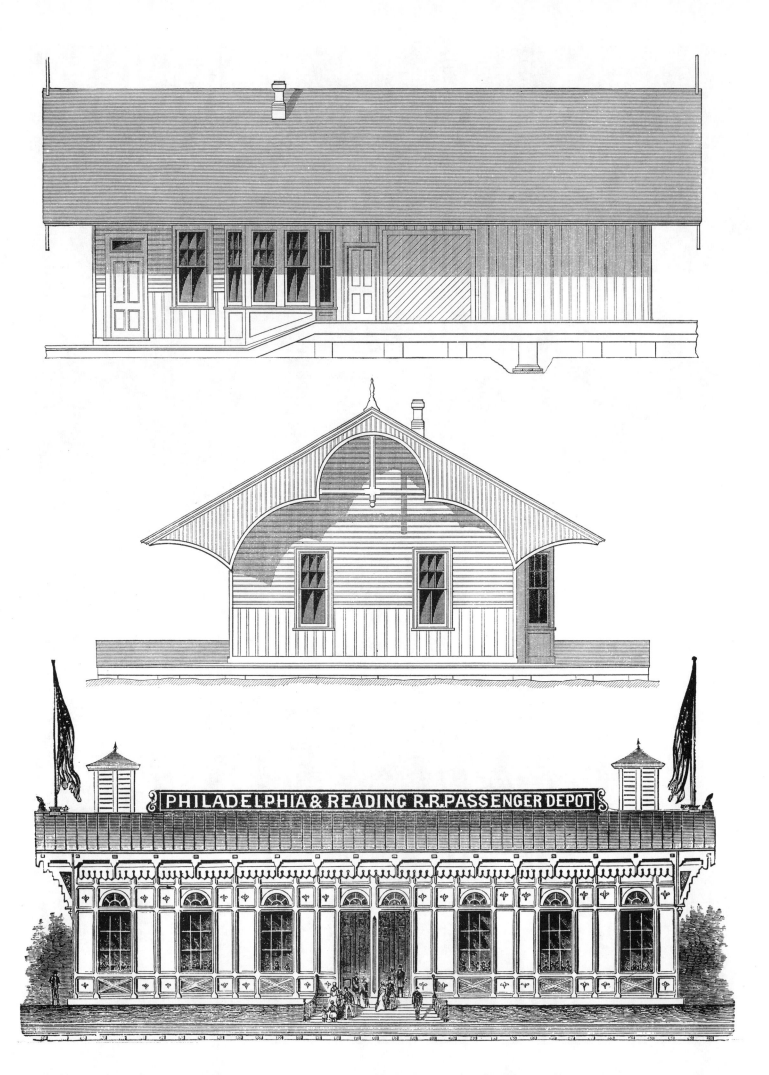

Top; Side elevation; combined freight and passenger depot, second class, South Florida R.R., 1886. Middle; End elevation of S.F. R.R. depot. Bottom; Centennial Depot, Philadelphia & Reading R.R., 1876.

Top; Station of Chicago, Milwaukee & St. Paul R.R., Milwaukee, 1887. Bottom; Union Depot, Pittsburgh, c.1877.

Bird's-eye view of Chicago rail passenger facilities, 1874. Included in area were terminals for the Michigan Southern and Rock Island railroads, Pittsburg, Ft. Wayne & Chicago R.R., Chicago, Alton & St. Louis R.R., and the Great Central Depot. The dark area in the picture is where the great fire had occurred.

Passenger depot for Michigan Southern and Rock Island railroads, Chicago, 1873.

Examples of what was commonly called "Railroad Gothic" architecture: Top; Union Railway Station, Pittsfield, Mass., 1876. Bottom; Illinois Central R.R. station, Jackson Park, Chicago, 1887.

Passenger stations in Worcester, Mass., c.1886: Top; Worcester & Shrewsbury R.R. Bottom; Union Railway Passenger Station.

Top; Union Depot, Leavenworth, Kans., c.1886. Bottom; Union Depot, Kansas City, Mo., c.1886.

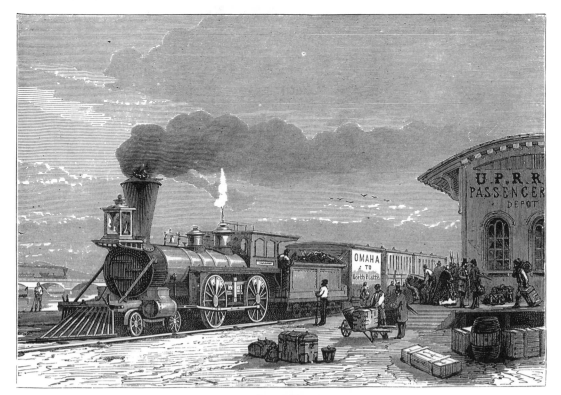

Union Pacific passenger stations in Omaha, Nebr.: Top; c.1869. Bottom; Early 1880s.

At the time railroads began in this country, mail service was in a primitive state, having to depend on the poor network of roads, and the slow methods of transportation available. Some mail moved either by sail or steamboat; otherwise it went by stage, post coach, carriage, or on horseback. The first mail to move by rail was carried on the Charleston & Hamburg Railroad in November 1831. The Baltimore & Ohio inaugurated its mail service on January 1, 1832. Shortly, both the Camden & Amboy Railroad and Saratoga & Schenectady Railroad began carrying mail on their trains as well. The official beginning of Railway Mail Service coincided with the inauguration of the B&O line between Washington, D.C., and Baltimore on August 25, 1835. Within the next two years rail mail service had become so successful that on July 7, 1838, Congress passed a law establishing every railroad in America as a post route.

Originally railroads were given sealed bags of mail that they put on any car having space. Later, special mail cars were added to trains. Technically, mail was freight, but the important need for giving it more expeditious service led to its being carried on passenger trains. The developments in American mail service that later followed were probably influenced by improvements made in England. In 1840 the first mail train ran in England, although it did carry a few passenger cars. Special cars were developed in the 1840s where mail might be sorted while the train was en route to its destination. By 1855 trains made up exclusively of mail cars were in operation, and a system was pioneered for catching bags of outgoing mail, hung up by stations along the way, without the train having to stop.

In the uncertainty of the first few months of the Civil War, trains continued to carry mail anywhere battles were not being fought. Afterward each side operated its mail service separately. In the early 1860s Colonel George B. Armstrong, assistant postmaster in Chicago, began promoting the idea of expediting service by sorting mail aboard moving trains. Following his lead, William A. Davis, assistant postmaster in St. Joseph, Missouri, persuaded the Hannibal & St. Joseph Railroad, a new line across Missouri, to try out this idea. A converted baggage car was equipped with a letter case and sorting shelf, and it began operation between West Quincy, Illinois, and St. Joseph, Missouri, on July 28, 1862. In 1864, under Colonel Armstrong's guidance, the Chicago & North Western Railroad started operating a similar car between Chicago and Clinton. In autumn of that year, the new U.S. Railway Post Office, a more elaborately equipped car, began operation between New York and Washington, D.C. It even had an exterior letter-deposit box so that anywhere along the car's route where it might be stopped, people could deposit important mail. The introduction of these cars was a great success. In 1869, when Congress created the Railway Mail Service, Colonel Armstrong became the first general superintendent.

In 1875 George S. Bangs, who succeeded Colonel Armstrong, persuaded William H. Vanderbilt, head of the New York Central Railroad, to create an all-mail express train that would operate between New York and Chicago. Vanderbilt, over the objection of his father, the Commodore, agreed to this and invested much time and money having cars built and designing a system to pick up mailbags, with a train in motion, at the more than one hundred way stations en route. On September 16, 1875, service of the *Fast Mail* was begun, and soon a similar train, the *Limited Mail,* began operation on the Pennsylvania Railroad between Philadelphia and Chicago; each train was scheduled to complete its trip in twenty-four hours. Though the trains were very successful, they did not survive the unexpected withdrawal of federal funds that occurred ten months later. Bangs was humiliated by this development and resigned. However, Congress renewed its funding in 1877 and both trains were returned to operation. Later, the Union Pacific began operating its own fast mail train, which, connecting with the other two, created a coast-to-coast fast mail service.

Although for a little while some glamour was attached to the jobs, working on Railway Post Office cars or Fast Mail trains was, perhaps like other railway jobs, long, exhausting, poorly paid, and occasionally dangerous. Mail cars were usually situated right behind the locomotive and tender; thus the clerks inside were particularly vulnerable in case of train collision or derailment. From 1876 to 1905 there were 9,355 accidents to mail-carrying trains. In these, 207 clerks were killed and 1,516 seriously injured. In the rather frequent train robberies of the time, mail cars were often the chief target. Finally, burglar- and collision-proof mail cars were developed about 1895. First running between New York and Chicago on the New York, Lake Erie & Western Railroad, these cars were sealed off from any contact with the rest of the train and given armored protection by the use of steel plates. Inside, they were better reinforced against damage from collisions, and beds, similar to ship berths, were provided for the clerks.

Mail was distributed over 126,310 miles of railway by 1888, with postal clerk crews traveling 122 million miles in performance of their work. Mail hauling continued to be a big part of railroad business until after World War II, when increasing amounts began going by truck or plane. The last RPO route was ended on July 1, 1977.

The new United States Railway Post Office, a rail car operating between New York and Washington D.C., 1864. Top left; Sorting papers. Top right; Sorting letters.
Bottom; General view of car interior.

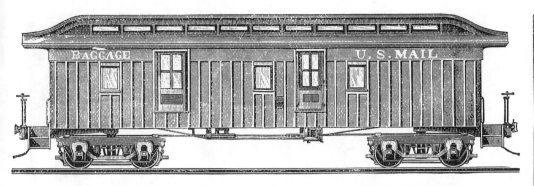

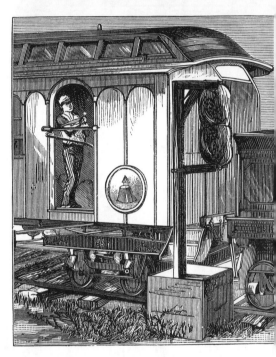

Top left; Combination mail and baggage car, c.1879. Top right; Catching mail at way stations, 1875. Middle left; Delivering newspapers, 1875. Middle right; Use of the catching hook, 1875. Bottom; Railway Post Office car, 1864.

Top; New York Central R.R. fast mail train at Grand Central Station, New York, 1875. Bottom; N.Y.C. R.R. fast mail engine No. 110 pulled trains between Syracuse and Buffalo attaining speeds of 65-75 mph., 1875.

Transfer of mail at Grand Central Station, New York, 1889.

The railway mail service methods of distributing and delivering the mail, 1888. Top; Before the start; delivering the mail and daily papers at the Pennsylvania Railway Depot at Jersey City. Middle; Interior of car; distributing mail. Bottom left; "Ready to throw off." Bottom right; "The catch."

Before the advent of railroads in this country, all freight shipments went either by wagon or by water. The revolution railroads brought in providing more direct routes, speed of service, and lowered cost was to totally change the realm of possibilities that existed in the business world of that time. Local and regional economies that were largely independent of one another slowly evolved into an interdependent national economy. Perishable agricultural products and other goods previously limited to these small regions could now be shipped almost anywhere. Regions could specialize more. Factories could be located further away from both their sources of raw materials and the consumers of their products, and their business could be conducted on a much vaster scale. One good example of this was the steel industry that grew up in Pittsburgh following the Civil War. Iron ore was shipped in from open pit mines in Minnesota and Michigan. The coal that fired the smelters came from western Pennsylvania and West Virginia. Often, the steel produced was then shipped to other factories elsewhere. Finally, after using it in the manufacture of their products, these companies might ship the finished goods across the country, or even overseas.

Rather early, railroad freight revenues began to exceed those for passenger service. By the mid 1850s this figure was about 20 percent greater. To a large extent railroads were prisoners in their own domain, being held captive by the economic potentials that existed in the regions they served. The Pennsylvania and New York Central lines, both in the enviable position of operating in areas of high population and rapid economic growth, became the nation's largest freight carriers. However, being in an area of fierce competition, they had to keep their rates relatively low. Lines in the Midwest had less competition and could maintain higher rates. However, they were vulnerable to the feast or famine fluctuations of agricultural cycles and the seasonal nature of the business, operating at maximum capacity during the grain harvest and having a light flow of traffic the rest of the year. Similarly, fortunes of other lines might be tied to coal, like the Philadelphia & Reading, Lehigh Valley, and Lackawanna railroads; to iron ore, like the Iron Mountain line, Duluth, Missabe & Northern line, and Duluth & Iron Range line; or to oil; as in the case of the Philadelphia & Erie and Atlantic & Great Western railroads. Elsewhere railways were largely dependent for their survival upon the transportation of livestock, timber, other agricultural products, or manufactured goods.

Typically freight trains were longer and traveled much slower than passenger trains. Different types of cars evolved to solve the problems posed by shipping different kinds of raw materials or products. Shipments of heavy unrefined ores needed no protection and might ride in a gondola. Perishable grain required protection from weather and usually rode in boxcars or covered hoppers. Furniture and other manufactured products also needed protection, and rode in a boxcar. Shipping a new combine, however, might require a flat car. Primitive forms of these types of cars all appeared in the 1830s or earlier. The first car designed for hauling oil, built in 1865, had mounted on a flat car two large, covered, round wooden tubs. Shortly, the type familiar today, with the horizontal cylinder tank, made its appearance.

After the Civil War, as more railroads adopted the standard gauge, car-interchange agreements were made allowing the cars of one line to be run over another. This led to a more unified system and saved much time. Previously, when changing lines, shipments had been unloaded by one railroad into wagons and then reloaded into the cars of another. Also about this time, the first refrigerated cars appeared. Fast freight companies became a new development, as well, following the war. These companies, often formed by cooperating railroads, consolidated shipments and provided expedited service for various kinds of freight. Among these companies were Great Western Dispatch, Green Line, Star Union, Merchants Dispatch, and Traders Dispatch.

Competition among lines was intense and railroads often resorted to rather underhanded tactics, either to gain advantage or merely to survive. Most typically they would cut rates where the competition required it and raise them elsewhere. In Pennsylvania competing lines published rates for shipping oil that only the small companies paid. They secretly granted generous rebates to the largest shipper, John D. Rockefeller's Standard Oil Company. In the Midwest, railroads often owned local grain elevators, frequently charging excessive storage rates. They also often downgraded grain at the point of purchase from the farmer and then upgraded it before selling it to the large milling companies. In 1870 the New York Central and Erie lines engaged in such fierce competition for hauling livestock from Buffalo to New York that finally the New York Central reduced its rate to one dollar a carload. This was a charge far below what it cost the line to move them, and the normal rate had been $160 per carload. Officials from the Erie then bought a substantial number of cattle and shipped them over the New York Central, hurting their competitor and making a handsome profit in the process. In Kansas, between 1867 and 1870, over a million head of cattle, mostly driven from Texas, were shipped east from Abilene on the Kansas Pacific Railroad. The Atchinson, Topeka & Santa Fe, perhaps observing this success, built a parallel line to the south; first to Newton, and then to Dodge City. It was successful in intercepting the Texas herds, and in doing so captured most of the Kansas Pacific's business.

The reverse side of rate wars was pooling. This practice was a secret and illegal collusion among competing railroads where they came to an agreement about dividing the spoils. Sometimes a revenue pool was held in common and then divided up. In other cases they each might agree to carry a certain percentage of the business. Some lines also colluded in dividing up territory, determining where they might extend lines and where they couldn't. These illegal practices eventually led to regulations by various state legislatures, and finally to the Interstate Commerce Act of 1887, which created the Interstate Commerce Commission.

Moving a string of empty box cars on the Illinois Central R.R., Chicago, 1868. In background is the Great Central Depot.

New Hudson River R.R. freight depot, corner of Laight and Hudson Streets, [former site of St. John's Park] Manhattan, 1869. Top; Main edifice featuring Commodore Vanderbilt. Bottom; View of part of building, shows "dummy" locomotive pulling boxcars.

Freight train crossing the Erie Canal in upstate New York; New York, West Shore & Buffalo R.R., 1873.

Foreign goods being unloaded at the Centennial Exposition, Philadelphia, 1876.

Grain elevator of the New York Central & Hudson River R.R., New York, 1877.

Top; Shipping cotton from Pine Bluff, Ark., 1879. Bottom; Loading watermelons for shipment, Atlanta, 1888.

Union Stockyards, Chicago, c.1880.

View of rail traffic at McCormick Reaper factory, Chicago, 1885.

Top; Coal depot at Port Carbon, Pa. Bottom; Departure of the "Corn Train" from Wichita, Kans., for the Ohio River valley; Atcheson, Topeka & Santa Fe R.R., 1884.

Henry Colliery of the Lehigh Valley Coal Co., Wilkes-Barre, Pa., 1887.

168

Top; Lumber mill scene, Pennsylvania, c.1887. Bottom; Logging railroad, c.1890.

Chicago freight yards, view from Lake Michigan, 1886.

New York Central & Hudson River R.R. freight yards, W. 65th St., New York, 1889.

Harvest hands en route to wheat fields in the northwest, waiting for a train to pick up their reapers, 1890.

Loading disassembled locomotives for export to Australia, Pennsylvania R.R., 1891.

Transportation of bridge girders over New York Central R.R., 1893. The panel shows plate girder type bridge as completed.

Troops and supplies being transloaded from railcars to ships, prior to invasion of Cuba, Tampa, Fla., 1898.

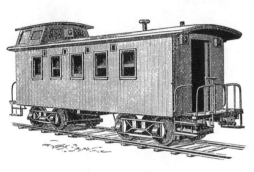

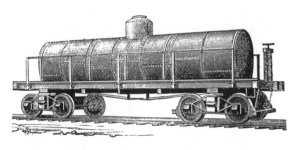

Top; Boxcar, c.1875. Upper middle left; caboose, c.1879. Lower middle left; tank car, c.1879. Bottom left; Boxcar, c.1890. Bottom right; Unloading cattle, 1868.

Top left; Cattle car, 1867. Top right; Canda cattle car, 1894. Middle right; Flat car, c.1879. Bottom; Livestock feeding and watering apparatus, 1880.

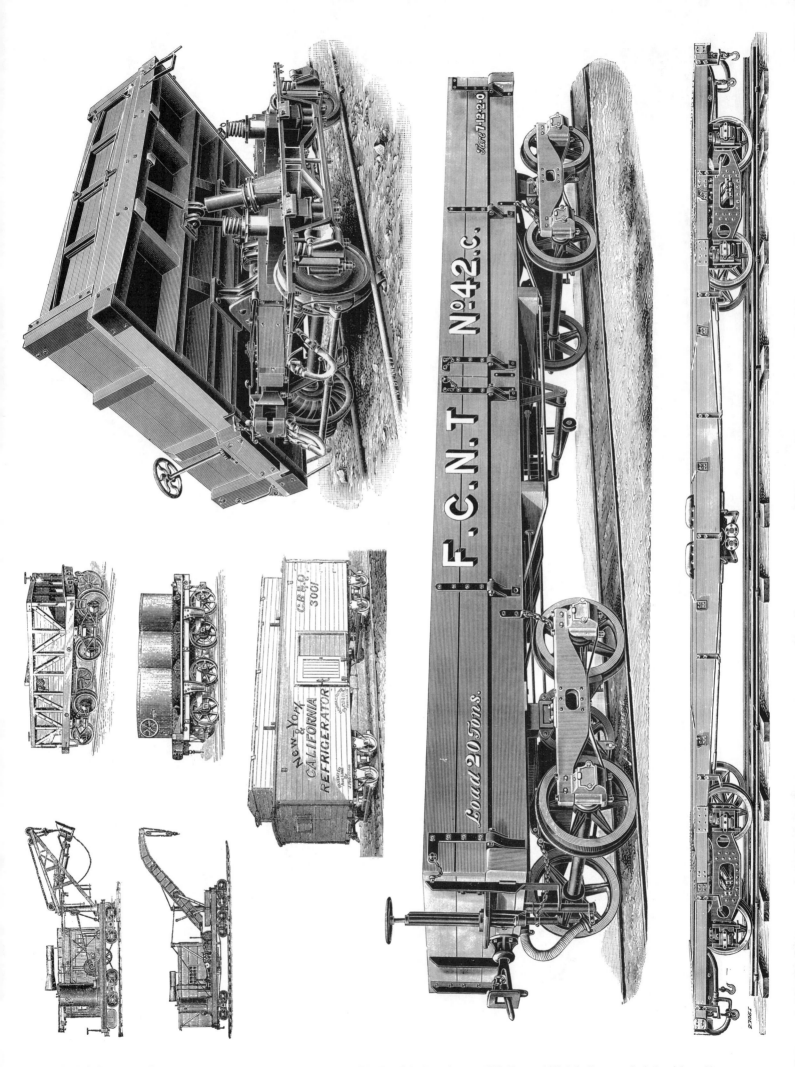

Top left; Steam shovel car for industrial use. Top center; Hopper car, c.1879. Top right; Dumping car, 1893. Upper middle left; Crane car for industrial use. Upper middle center; Iron-hopper coal car, c.1879. Middle center; Refrigerator car, 1870. Lower middle; Gondola, 1894. Bottom; Flat car, 1894.

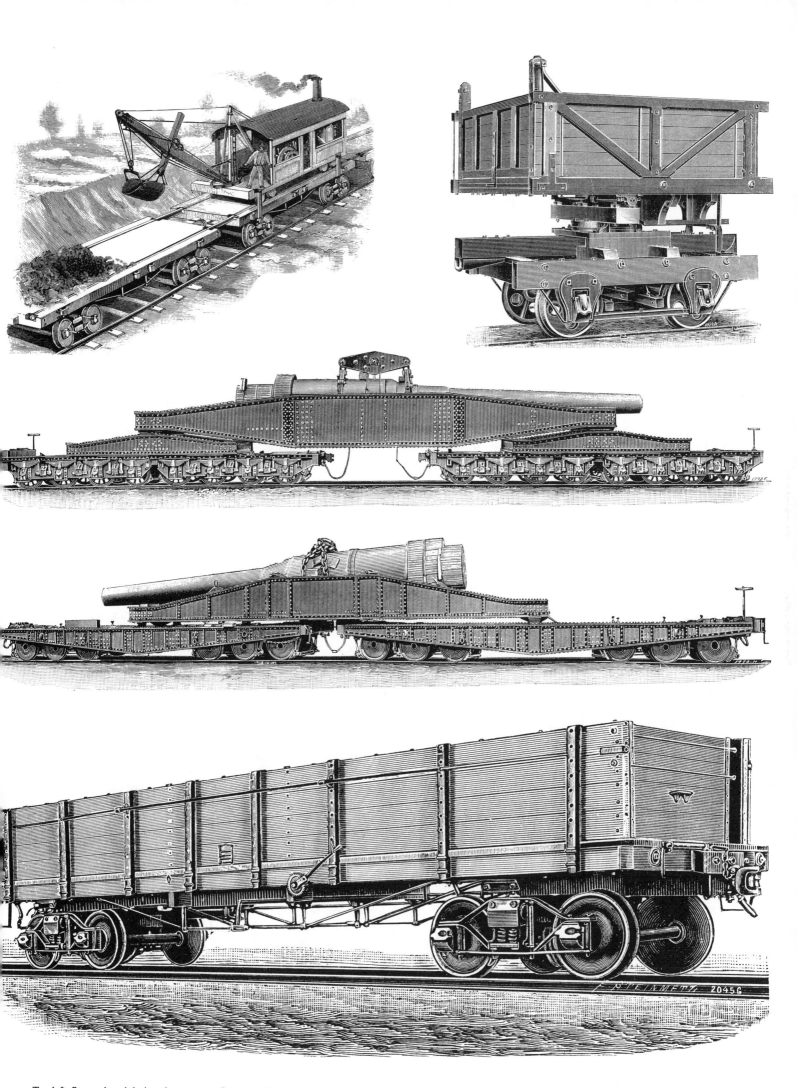

Top left; Steam shovel designed to move on flat cars, 1894. Top right; Rotary dump car, 1893. Middle; Pennsylvania R.R. cars for transporting heavy Krupp artillery to the Columbian Exposition in 1893. Upper; 120-ton gun. Lower; 62-ton gun. Bottom; Canda sliding bottom gondola, 1894.

The chief officers of a typical nineteenth-century railroad would usually be the president, secretary, and treasurer. A general manager would be in charge of running the operations of the railroad. Railroads covering some hundreds of miles were broken up into divisions. These were separated by towns or cities called division points, which often were located at important junction sites. Division points were approximately one hundred miles from each other, this being the average distance that a freight train might travel in a day. Division points became centers of activity for the railroads, and usually had a roundhouse, a repair shop, and a yard. In the yard arriving trains might be broken down, using switch engines, and the cars switched to a number of tracks having different destinations and priorities. As other cars were added to these tracks, new trains would gradually be formed. In the yard also, empty cars and maintenance equipment like cranes, snowplows, and work cars were sometimes kept. Train crews and other employees normally lived close by in these railroad towns, as they might be called up at any time for duty. It was typical for rail employees to work six days a week and ten to twelve hours a day. It was also common for train crews to work much longer on occasion, or otherwise get only a few hours of sleep before being called back to work. This proved occasionally to have disastrous consequences, but hours of service regulations weren't legislated until 1907.

Under the general manager might be division superintendents, a chief dispatcher, a master mechanic, a master car builder, and a track master. Under a division superintendent might be a yard master, repair shop supervisor, and roundhouse foreman. Working below these people in the yard, shop, and roundhouse would be many other employees: switchmen, switch-engine crews, repair and maintenance personnel, clerks, and so on. Under a chief dispatcher might be station agents, telegraph operators, and men in the switch and signal towers. Each division had its own dispatcher, who operated under a working schedule that fixed the position and time of all the trains moving on the line. Trains were assigned priority at various levels in a hierarchy that favored passengers, mail, and perishable freight like cattle or refrigerated foods. Thus, to accommodate scheduling, a slow-moving coal or work train would be moved to a siding, allowing an express or mail train from either direction to pass by. Double-track systems had existed as early as the 1840s but were rare throughout the nineteenth century. Delays and breakdowns were common and usually tended to affect the movement of other trains. It was the dispatcher's job, despite these obstacles, to somehow orchestrate all the trains safely to their destinations, with a minimum of inconvenience and lost time. The widespread adoption of telegraphic dispatching by the 1870s, and the somewhat synchronous development of manual semaphore signaling systems, followed later by automatic block signals, helped to make his job a little easier.

Train crews consisted of a conductor, an engineer, a fireman, and a number of brakemen. The conductor was in charge of the train and was under the supervision of the dispatcher, who provided him with written "train orders." Conductors were required to do all the paperwork for a trip. Passenger conductors dealt with the public, took the tickets, handled money, constantly checked the time to maintain the schedule, and signaled the engineer to resume the journey after making each stop. Freight conductors rode in the caboose at the rear of the train and watched it for any signs of trouble. After airbrakes were adopted—widely by 1890—conductors also monitored a gauge in the caboose for signs of any drop in air pressure. The paperwork of a freight train was considerable and listed every car on the train, the company, the number, where it was picked up and dropped off, and more. Typically a freight conductor had been promoted from being a brakeman and could hope for a promotion to passenger conductor.

Although on an equal pay scale with conductors, the engineers were subject to their direction. The engineer operated the locomotive and had to know the route with all of its bends, curves, grades, signals, bridges, tunnels, blind spots, and stops. Because the time required for braking was so long, especially before air brakes, engineers had to be constantly alert for any signs of danger. Before attaining the position of engineer, a person first had to serve as a fireman. The primary job of the fireman was throwing wood and, later, shoveling coal, into the firebox, in an effort to maintain the steam pressure at a desirable level. Firemen also were responsible for taking on water at water towers, lubricating the engine, watching its gauges, and during the few decades when it was fashionable, polishing the locomotive and tender to a high shine.

The entry-level job for train-crew service was that of brakeman, which, before the adoption of air brakes, was a perilous occupation. During those years, in making stops, the engineer might reverse the motion of his drivers, but the only brakes were on the individual cars, with each having to be applied separately by turning a wheel. At the whistle signal from the locomotive of "down brakes," the brakemen at various points on the train would immediately begin jumping from car to car and tightening the brake wheels until completing their sector. To release the brakes, another signal was given and the process was reversed. While riding on the top of a boxcar, a brakeman would have to watch for the approach of tunnels and low bridges. In darkness, bad weather, and on fast trains, his job often became treacherous, and many brakemen fell off, frequently to their death. In the late 1880s train deaths resulting from the falls of crewmen averaged approximately a thousand a year. Brakemen at the front and rear of trains had the added duties of functioning as switchmen and flagmen. When connecting or disconnecting cars with the link and pin coupling devices, they risked the additional danger of having fingers sheared off. Automatic couplers, first invented in 1867, were not widely used until the 1890s. Once trains were equipped with air brakes, the number of brakemen on freight crews was reduced, and those on passenger trains were assigned other duties.

Train crews made up only about 40 percent of the total employees of a railroad. Other employees included section hands responsible for inspecting and maintaining tracks and road bed; work crews that handled major repair jobs on the line, built bridges, or extended new branches; clerks of all kinds; maintenance people; station masters, baggage masters, and other station employees; call boys who rounded up crews for work; and railway postal employees. Soon after the turn of the century, in 1910, America had 1,699,420 people with railroad-related jobs.

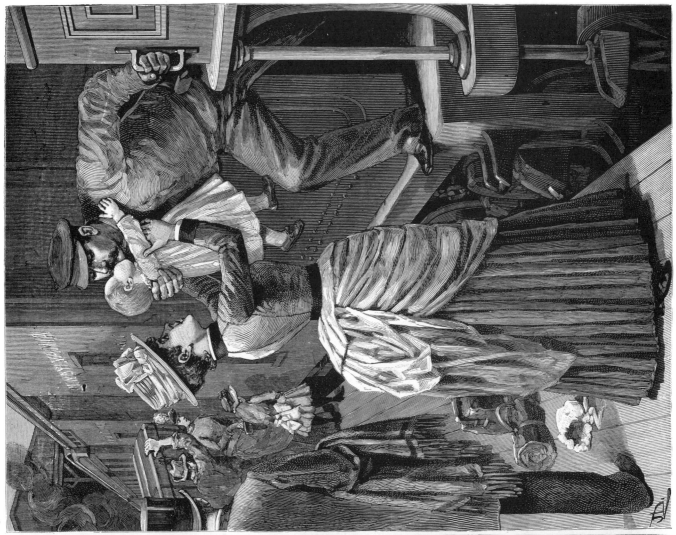

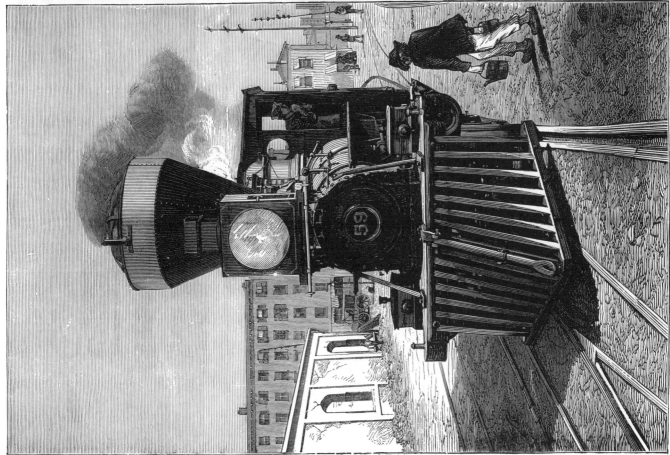

Left; Fireman hauling water to locomotive, 1873. **Right;** "The Good Bye Kiss," wife and child seeing off the engineer, 1889.

Top; Train at water tower, c.1889. Bottom; Erie train taking on water, 1874.

Engineer leans out to read signals ahead, c.1889.

Top; Conductor waking sleeping passenger to check tickets. Bottom; Brakeman in freight yard at night, c.1889.

Top left; Freight train brakeman in winter, 1877. Top right; Engineer, 1874. Middle center; Conductor. Middle right; Conductor, 1874. Bottom; Fighting fire at roundhouse in Galion, Ohio; Bellefontaine & Indianapolis R.R., 1866.

Switchman on nighttime duty at the approach to Philadelphia's Broad St. Station, Pennsylvania R.R., 1886.

Top; A flagman at a city train crossing. Bottom; An operator receiving the train staff, New York, New Haven & Hartford R.R., 1891.

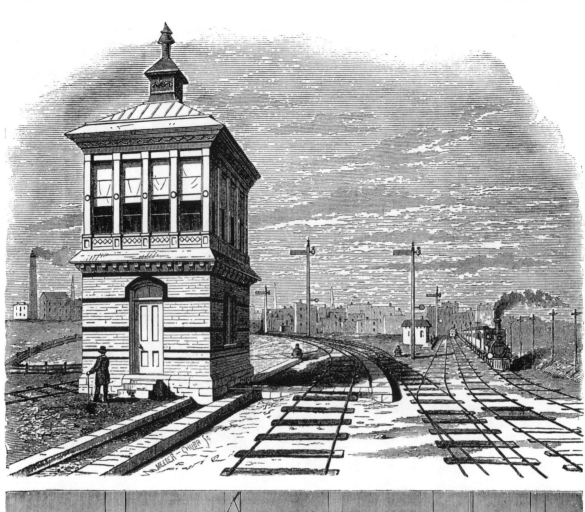

Top; Signal tower, switches and signals, 1875. Bottom; Saxby and Farmer system of safety switches and signals, 1875.

Top; Block signal station, Pennsylvania R.R. Bottom; New Westinghouse automatic block system on the Central Railroad of New Jersey, 1890.

Mantua Junction, West Philadelphia, showing a complex system of interlacing tracks.

Inspection cars, Pennsylvania R.R.: Top; 1891. Bottom; 1882.

Construction or "work" trains: Top; Train in Montana; St. Paul, Minneapolis & Manitoba Rwy., which later became the Great Northern R.R., 1887. Bottom; Train in Virginia; Norfolk & Western R.R., 1885.

Railroad work crew operating a grader, 1877.

Work crew operating a ballast crushing machine, 1893.

Combined steam shovel and derrick car, Northern Pacific R.R., 1883.

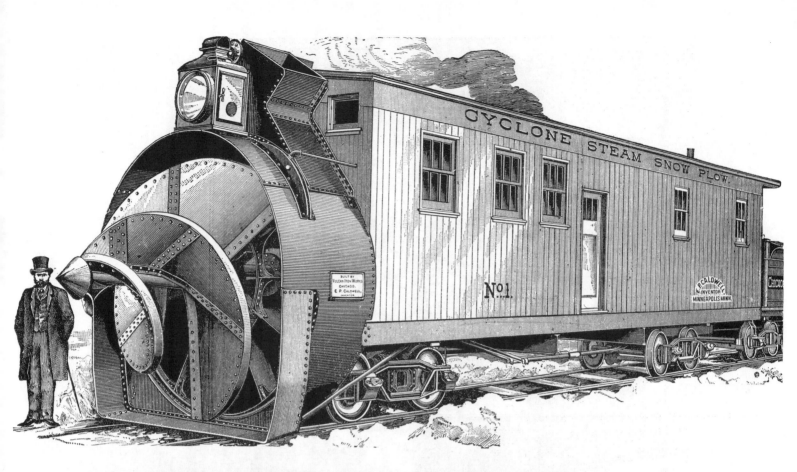

Heavy equipment for line maintenance: Top; Cyclone steam snow plow, 1889. Bottom; Abbiati snow plow and track cleaner in operation, Union Pacific R.R., 1874.

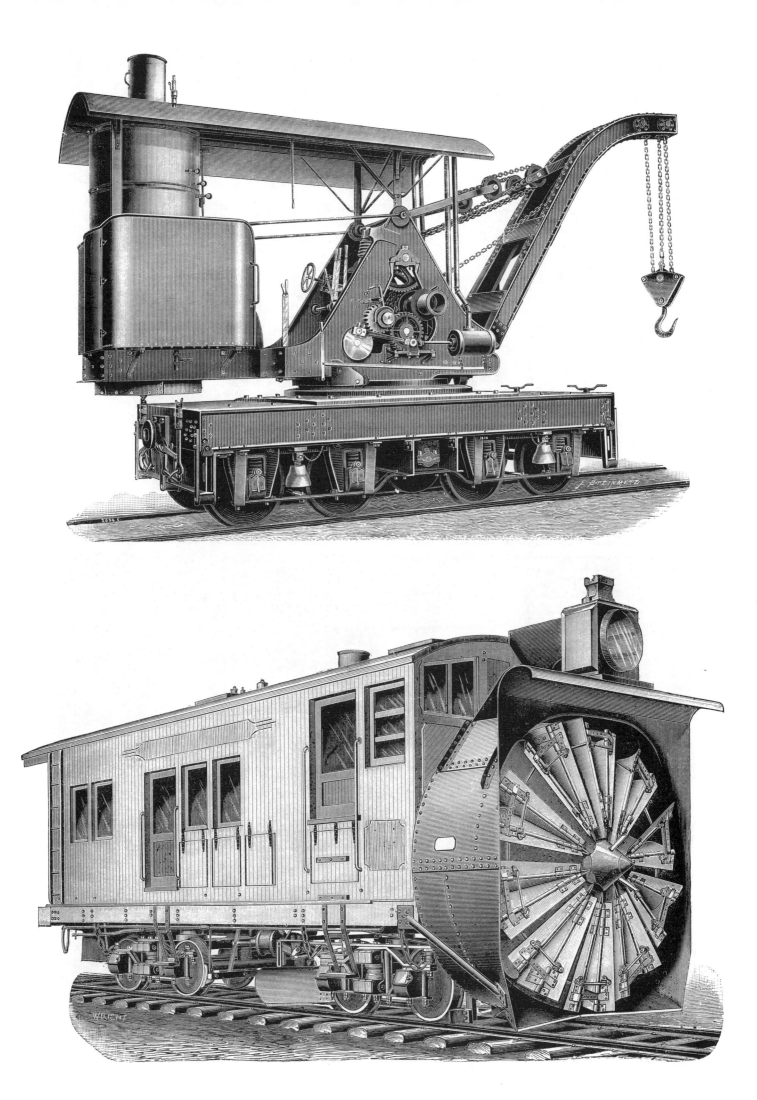

Heavy equipment for line maintenance: Top; 15-ton locomotive crane, 1893. Bottom; Rotary steam snow plow, 1893.

Section hands in a push car going down for provisions, the Continental Divide, 1889.

Handcars: Top left; Cyrus Roberts Co., 1893. Top right; The Buda Co., 1889. Middle right; Car, c.1900. Bottom; Steam inspection car, M.M. Buck Co., 1876.

10 · RAILROAD LABOR DISPUTES

In the early 1870s, after disclosures of financial and stock manipulations, rate gouging, and bribery, the public attitude toward railroads became increasingly distrustful. In the Midwest, after suffering abuse for many years from a railway monopoly controlling the grain traffic, farmers organized for action. Soon a rapidly growing Grange movement overcame railroad power in the state legislatures, and laws were passed regulating railroad freight, passenger, and storage rates.

Railroad workers themselves became increasingly dissatisfied as their employers changed work rules in an effort to extract more performance. Following the panic of 1873, many lines cut employee wages, and other reductions followed for the next few years. As this happened, however, the cost of living remained the same. During this period the labor supply was plentiful due to the large immigration from Europe. Employees might have felt dissatisfied, but there was little they could do. Furthermore, the existing unions, like the Brotherhood of Locomotive Engineers, were mainly social and fraternal groups, and not set up for voicing grievances.

Although small labor disputes had occurred in the past, the year 1877 was to bring something entirely new. That year the average salary for engineers and conductors was $3 a day; for firemen $2; and for brakemen $1.75. About this time the New York Central, Baltimore & Ohio, Pennsylvania, and Erie railroads set up a railroad pool, where they colluded on rates and collectively agreed to reduce wages as well. On June 1, the Pennsylvania Railroad announced cuts of 10 percent. It was followed by the New York Central as well as other lines like the Lackawanna, Lehigh Valley, and Michigan Central. On July 1, the Erie slashed its wages, and the B&O, having made a previous cut only eight months earlier, followed on July 16.

While the employees of the other lines had continued work, strikes began immediately on the B&O, with the firemen and brakemen initiating the action. All traffic stopped moving at Martinsburg, West Virginia, and the state militia was called in. There was much public sympathy for the strikers and the militia proved ineffective. Federal troops were sent by President Rutherford B. Hayes; upon their arrival, they fired into a crowd of strikers, killing ten people.

Word of this incident quickly spread to other cities, igniting protests in such faraway places as Buffalo, Omaha, St. Louis, and St. Paul. In Baltimore an angry crowd gathered at Camden Station and was fired upon by soldiers armed with Gatling guns. In Chicago the protest degenerated into a general civil insurrection with armed groups of thugs, looters, and arsonists doing much destruction.

The worst violence, however, broke out in Pittsburgh on the Pennsylvania line. As the protest expanded, police, sheriffs deputies, armed Pinkerton strikebreakers, state militia, and finally federal troops were all called in. In the course of this rampage, over one hundred locomotives and two thousand cars were destroyed; and Union Station, various company offices, and the roundhouse were burned. There were also many reports of arson and looting elsewhere in the city. Thousands of people were hurt and about twenty-five people were killed. It took ten thousand troops to get the railroad in operation once more.

Though there was considerable sympathy in this country for the workers, the riots did much to dispel it. Afterward, thousands of railroad employees involved in the strikes were fired and blacklisted. However, this experience led to a greater solidarity on the part of the workers, and railroads became a little more cautious in doing things to aggravate them. Union activities continued to increase in the 1880s and 1890s, and there were occasionally small strikes and disputes. In 1883 the Trainmen's Union was established. This was followed by the Order of Railroad Telegraphers in 1887, and the Brotherhood of Railway Carmen in 1891.

In 1893, Eugene V. Debs, previously a secretary of the Brotherhood of Railroad Firemen, organized the American Railway Union and led a successful strike against the Great Northern line. After the Pullman Company in Chicago cut its wages, Debs called a strike, instructing all his union members to walk off their jobs on any railroad carrying Pullman cars. President Grover Cleveland, called upon to intervene, sent federal troops into Chicago. Rioting erupted there and twelve died before the strike was broken on July 19. Debs was among many who were arrested. He later ran unsuccessfully five times for the U.S. presidency as a Socialist party candidate.

Although this strike ended up much like that of 1877, it did indicate the growing power of the labor movement as the nineteenth century waned. During this period, workers, farmers, and other reform-minded individuals joined together in the populist movement and took over the Democratic party, running William Jennings Bryan for president in 1896. In 1894 the Switchman's Union was established, and in 1898 the Brotherhood of Railway and Steamship Clerks, Freight Handlers, Express, and Station Employees followed.

Top; Erie strikers stopping express train, Susquehanna, Pa., 1874. Bottom; Strike on the Central Railroad of New Jersey; A Pennsylvania R.R. engine crashes barrier at a junction of the two lines, 1876.

The great railway strike of 1877: Top; Blockade of engines at Martinsburg, W.Va. early in the strike, Baltimore & Ohio R.R. Bottom; Police beating back strikers in Philadelphia, Pennsylvania R.R., July 23.

The great railway strike of 1877: Destruction of the Union Depot and Hotel, Pittsburgh.

The great railway strike of 1877: Steeple view of burning trains at Pittsburgh.

Strike on the Gould Railway System: The crew of a freight train in Marshall, Tex. abandoning their locomotive at the command of strikers, Missouri Pacific R.R., 1885.

A train, guarded by U.S. Marshals, attempts starting during a strike, East St. Louis, Ill., 1886.

Starting of the first suburban train in Chicago after a strike of engineers, Chicago, Burlington & Quincy R.R., 1888.

11 • BRIDGES AND TUNNELS

The general practice in railroading from the beginning was to lay out the course of the line in such a manner that grades and curves would be as gentle as possible. It was seen that any deviation from dead level or from a straight line was uneconomical from the standpoint that there would be an additional cost in time, in consumption of fuel, and in wear and tear on the equipment. In cases of sudden loss in elevation, such as encountering a creek or river bed, a bridge would be required. In cases of sudden increase in elevation, as where a mountain couldn't easily be built around, the obstacle would have to be tunneled through instead. Tunnels were also occasionally constructed beneath rivers, or as in the case of the New York subway system, begun in 1900, built when there was too much competition for the space above.

The simplest bridges are beam bridges, and these are used even up to the present for short spans up to thirty-five or forty feet; multiple spans may be constructed to extend the lengths where the foundation is suitable for supporting piers. Wooden trestles were for many years the most common type of bridge, as they were the least expensive; however, they were always considered a temporary or semipermanent solution at best, because they would eventually rot and were also vulnerable to fire. Covered bridges were occasionally built up to the time of the Civil War. Stone bridges were more permanent, but they had a tendency to settle.

The first iron bridge was built in 1840 over the Erie Canal by Earl Trumbell. That same year Squire Whipple built the first bowstring truss and published a study on stresses in bridge trusses. In 1845 the first iron-truss railroad bridge was built on the Philadelphia and Reading line. Using trusses, the length of possible spans increased remarkably and by early in this century had reached 720 feet. When John Augustus Roebling invented the wire cable, long suspension bridges became possible. The engineering profession was very skeptical of this new technique, but Roebling prevailed. The first wire-cable suspension bridge opened in May 1845 to span the Allegheny River at Pittsburgh. The International Suspension Bridge near Niagara Falls was begun in 1852 and opened in 1856.

In their book, *Railways: The Pioneer Years,* Malcolm Fletcher and John Taylor state:

There are three types of river-bed which the bridge builder will encounter. In some cases, the river-bed is made of hard rock and can bear heavy loads without any chance of erosion. Frequently, the river-bed is made of gravel, pebbles, sand, compacted clay or tuff. Again such ground cannot be compressed further and will carry heavy loads. There is, however, a possibility that it may shift. Basically, if the land is peat or mud, it can be eroded and will not support a heavy load. In such cases, the foundations have to be sunk down until they reach a solid base. Where this method proves impractical, compressible soil can still be built on. This is done by increasing the surface size of the base so that the pressure the soil must withstand is reduced.

In the long run permanent bridges were always safer and more economical than the temporary ones; nonetheless into the 1880s it remained the policy of most railroads to prefer the short-term solution. In the year 1888, America had 61,562 iron and wooden truss bridges and 147,187 wooden trestles. From 1877 to 1887 there had been 251 bridge collapses. After this period, however, there was more of a move toward higher-quality bridge building. Besides the International Suspension Bridge, other remarkable American bridges include what is currently the world's oldest, the Carrollton Viaduct, a beautiful stone bridge crossing the Patapsco River at Relay, Maryland, built in 1829 on the B&O Railroad; the Starrucca Viaduct near Susquehanna, Pennsylvania, which opened in 1847 on the Erie line and had seventeen bluestone arches; the wooden Erie Railroad bridge crossing the Genesee River at Portage, New York, which opened in 1852; the steel-arched Eads Bridge across the Mississippi River at St. Louis, inaugurated in 1874; and the Pennsylvania Railroad bridge across the Hudson River at Poughkeepsie, which opened in 1889.

The first American railroad tunnel was built at Staple Bend, Pennsylvania, on the Allegheny Portage Railroad and opened in 1834. Compared to bridges, tunnels were an even more expensive undertaking and were avoided as much as possible until railroads began crossing the Alleghenies about 1850. Sometimes less expensive cuts were made rather than tunnels, but they had certain disadvantages of their own; softer debris from the top tended to fall to the bottom, rocks or small boulders could fall on passing trains, and cuts tended to fill with snow in the winter. One early tunnel in the Alleghenies, the Kingwood Tunnel on the B&O, was 4,100 feet long and took three years to complete. Unfortunately the roof didn't hold well and it was closed in 1855. A really gigantic project, the Hoosac Tunnel in Massachusetts, was begun in 1851 and only completed, after many starts and stops, in 1875. It was four and a half miles in length and cost over 17 million dollars. Later, when the railroads entered the Rocky Mountains and Sierra Nevadas, many more tunnels had to be built.

Railroad tunnel construction didn't differ much from the traditional practices employed in digging mines, but with tunnels both grade and alignment were more critical. Once the hole was being dug, strong timbers were used to provide temporary support for the roof. Compressed-air drilling and nitroglycerin explosives, both introduced about 1870, made tunneling a somewhat easier task. Improvements were also made in the techniques and materials used in providing interior support for tunnels.

The Tray Run Viaduct, Baltimore & Ohio R.R., 1861.

Bridge across the Hudson River at Albany; Hudson River R.R., 1866.

Top; Bridge across the Genesee River, Portage, N.Y., New York, Lake Erie & Western R.R., 1866. Bottom; International Suspension Bridge, near Niagara Falls, N.Y., 1866.

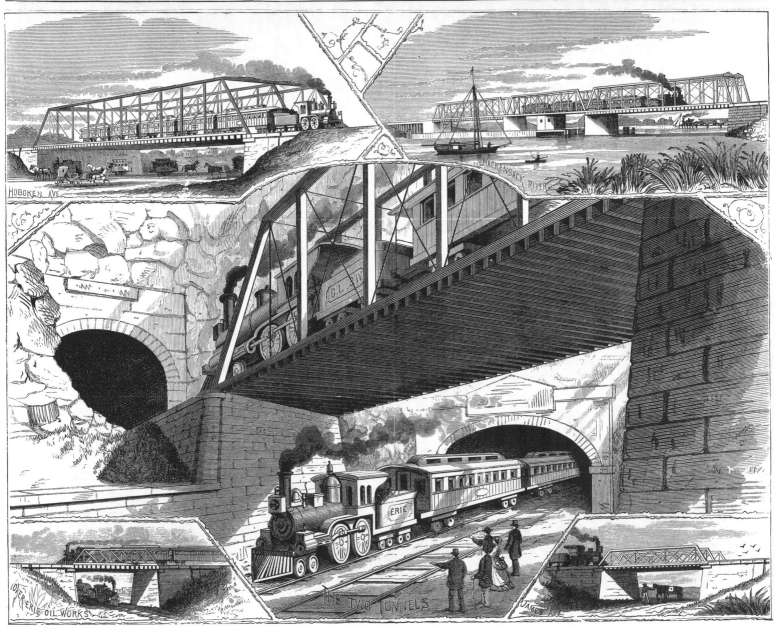

Top; Bridge over the Mississippi River, Brainerd, Minn., Northern Pacific R.R., 1871. Bottom; Engineering works of the Delaware, Lackawanna & Western R.R., 1877.

Top; Bridge across the Schuylkill River, West Philadelphia, Pa., 1876. Bottom; Bridge over the Delaware River, Yardleyville, N.J., 1876.

Top; Eads Bridge across the Mississippi River, St. Louis, Mo., opened 1874. Bottom; Howe truss bridge over Ashtabula Creek, Ohio; Lake Shore R.R., c.1876.

Lifting bridge for double-track railway over Oswego Canal, Syracuse, N.Y., New York, West Shore & Buffalo R.R., 1883. Top; Raised. Bottom; Lowered.

Bismarck Bridge over the Missouri River, Bismarck, N. Dak., Northern Pacific R.R., c.1883.

Top; Section of Bergen Tunnel lined with Beton; New York, Lake Erie & Western R.R., c.1878. Bottom; Laying iron plates, Hudson River railroad tunnel between New Jersey and Manhattan, 1880.

The First Train

Masonry at Entrance

A Segment

Tunnel Entrance.

Nº 1736 Where Beach Shields came together.

Where Tunnel crosses St. Clair River

The great railway tunnel under the St. Clair River, between the United States and Canada, 1891.

12 · THE HAZARDS OF RAIL TRAVEL

ollowing the Civil War, train travel in America entered an increasingly risky phase, having its roots in such causes as increased traffic, heavier equipment, rapid expansion of lines, reluctance of some railroads to use telegraphs or adapt other safety practices, and perhaps an increased willingness to confront the forces of nature while moving passengers and freight to their destination. All kinds of things, from the trivial to the tragic, might happen to distract the traveler from the pleasant reveries of his journey. There were always dangers from mechanical breakdown, derailments, unsafe bridges, and human error, but nature also occasionally provided problems. In an age when few streams or rivers were dammed, floods were frequent and often washed out tracks or bridges. During winter months, snowstorms in the North and West stranded many trains, often for days, and crews and passengers alike sometimes had to improvise to stay alive. Following severe blizzards, the haunting illustrations of such stranded trains might appear in *Harper's Weekly* or *Frank Leslie's Illustrated Newspaper* and were occasionally published in Europe as well. Snowplows—first the wedge, then the wing, and finally the rotary—were used in an increasingly successful effort to keep the tracks clear. The Central Pacific Railroad pioneered the use of snow sheds in the Sierra Nevada Mountains, but they were later discovered to be a fire hazard. Other lines tried the use of snow fences.

In rare instances trains encountered still other natural forces, braving prairie and forest fires, severe winds and sandstorms, lightning, and, in an incident recorded in the November 1, 1890, issue of *Scientific American,* a tornado:

The most extraordinary feature of the storm was the overturning of an entire [Chicago & North Western] railroad train, consisting of three baggage cars and nine heavy sleeping coaches. The locomotive and tender alone remained on the track. The through passenger train arrived at the town of Fargo at the same time as the tornado. As the roofs of the railroad machine shop and freight house were carried away, the engineer thought it safer to move out of the station, but was compelled to stop at the crossing of the Chicago, Milwaukee & St. Paul Railroad. He found great difficulty in getting started again, and was moving along very slowly, when suddenly the whole train was turned over. The rate at which they were proceeding was so slow that none of the passengers was seriously injured, although the fright and the nervous and physical shock was very great. Had the train been running at an ordinary rate of speed the consequences would have been very frightful.

Beginning about the end of the Civil War, a new danger appeared to beset the train crews and passengers. As railroads gained control over most of the transportation business, including the shipment of gold, money, and other valuables, they began to be targeted by thieves who previously had preyed on stagecoaches. Perhaps also, the violence prevalent during the Civil War had become a habit that for some was not easily broken. In the first recorded incident, on May 5, 1865, a group presumed to be former Confederate irregulars derailed an Ohio & Mississippi Railroad train near Cincinnati and made off with the loot, crossing the Ohio River in small boats. On October 18, 1866, another Ohio & Mississippi train was robbed near Seymour, Indiana, with the thieves entering the express car from the passenger car immediately behind it. They took thirteen thousand dollars, a considerable sum at that time, and then, pulling the bell cord that signaled the engineer to stop, they made good their escape. About a year later in the same area, another train was hit by the Reno Brothers Gang, and John Reno was shortly captured and sent to prison. The gang was indicted for the October 18, 1866, robbery but no one was ever tried. The remaining Reno brothers and other accomplices robbed a number of other trains on the Cincinnati, Hamilton & Dayton and Ohio & Mississippi lines. When three gang members were finally captured by lawmen, they were seized by vigilantes and hung. Later, in November 1868, the remaining three brothers and one accomplice were captured and jailed at New Albany, Indiana. Vigilantes subsequently raided the jail and hung this group as well.

One of the most successful of the train-robbing gangs that followed was led by Jesse James. This group, which included his brother Frank, was mostly made up of veterans of Quantrill's irregular forces who had fought in Kansas and Missouri. Operating mainly in this same area, they began by robbing banks and stagecoaches. The first train robbery attributed to this gang occurred at Adair, Iowa, in 1873. There, a rope tied to a loosened rail was pulled at the last minute, causing a derailment and the death of the engineer. The safe was then looted and the passengers were robbed. On December 12, 1874, the gang stopped a train near Muncie Siding, Kansas, and successfully made off with $30,000 in gold dust, $20,000 in cash, and about $5,000 in jewelry. Subsequent holdups included trains near Otterville, Missouri; Glendale, Missouri; Winston, Missouri; and Blue Cut, Missouri. The James Gang exempted the Chicago, Burlington & Quincy Railroad from their misdeeds as the line, perhaps in a preemptive move, had given James's mother a free railroad pass. Jesse was killed on April 3, 1882, by the Ford brothers, recent recruits to the gang who had decided to cash in on his reward bounty. Although there were many other train robberies, an ever growing sophistication on the part of the railroads and the Pinkerton Agency in thwarting or solving them, eventually caused most criminals to turn their activities elsewhere.

Warning of danger ahead, 1872.

Placing alarm torpedoes to warn an approaching train of danger ahead, Pennsylvania R.R., 1885.

A lightning express train strikes a torpedo alarm, 1882.

Train halted before washed out bridge, 1869.

Train attempting to go through flood in Louisiana; New Orleans & Mobile R.R., 1881.

Trains attempting to go through floods: Top; Traversing the submerged Wabash Valley, 1858. Middle; In Wisconsin, 1881. Bottom; Near Pittston, Pa. 1878.

Sufferings in a snowstorm, Michigan Central R.R., 1864.

Top; Trying to dig out of snow, 1866. Bottom; Passenger train in snowstorm racing prairie fire, 1867.

Attempting to dig out stalled train, Central Pacific R.R., early 1870s.

Passenger train caught in snowdrifts, Dakota Territory; Northern Pacific R.R., 1886.

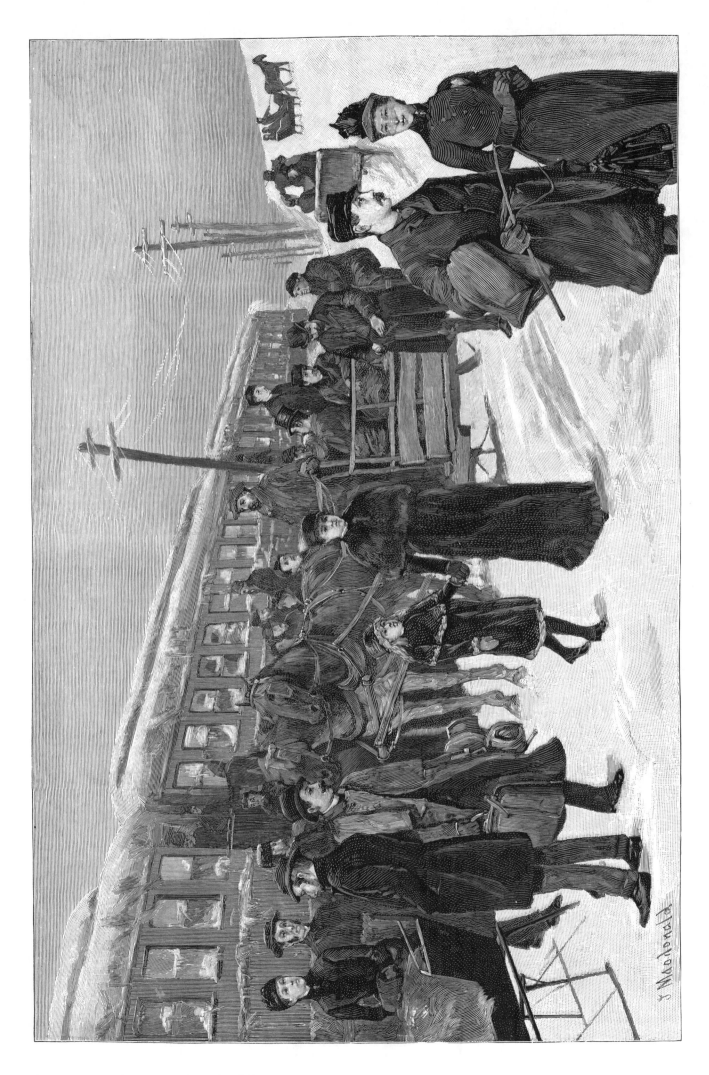

Stalled passenger train on the Canadian border, 1888.

Top; Train pushing snowplow through blizzard, c.1878. Bottom; Passengers taken from snowbound train to nearby town, 1886.

Rotary snowplow brings rescuers to stalled train; Union Pacific R.R., 1890.

Train in Oklahoma going through burning oil, Missouri, Kansas & Texas R.R., 1884.

Top; Train overturned by tornado at Fargo, N. Dak., Chicago & North Western R.R., 1890. Bottom; Train in severe sandstorm in eastern Oregon, Southern Pacific R.R., 1887.

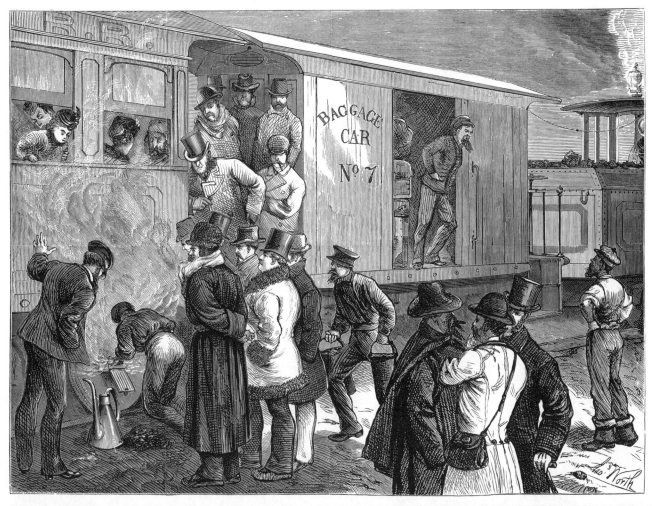

Top; Train stopped for "hot box" repair, 1874. Bottom; Fire in locomotive, Jersey City; Pennsylvania R.R., 1882.

"The Modern Dick Turpin," 1892. Illustration of a typical railroad holdup, making reference to an infamous English highwayman of an earlier time who finally was brought to the gallows.

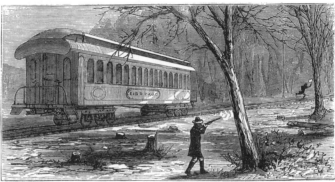

Top and middle; Robbery of a train at Muncie Siding, Kans., by the James Gang; Kansas Pacific R.R., Dec. 12, 1874. Top; Brigands compel the storekeeper to flag the train. Middle left; Section men forced to obstruct the track. Middle right; The conductor being fired upon. Bottom; "Dastardly attempt to destroy an express train on the St. Louis & San Francisco R.R., near Woodend Station, June 2, 1877."

$18,000.00 REWARD

Union Pacific Railroad and Pacific Express Companies jointly, will pay $2,000.00 per head, dead or alive, for the six robbers who held up Union Pacific mail and express train ten miles west of Rock Creek Station, Albany County, Wyoming, on the morning of June 2nd, 1899.

The United States Government has also offered a reward of $1,000.00 per head, making in all $3,000.00 for each of these robbers.

Three of the gang described below, are now being pursued in northern Wyoming; the other three are not yet located, but doubtless soon will be.

DESCRIPTION: One man about 32 years of age; height, five feet, nine inches; weight 185 pounds; complexion and hair, light; eyes, light blue; peculiar nose, flattened at bridge and heavy at point; round, full, red face; bald forehead; walks slightly stooping; when last seen wore No. 8 cow-boy boots.

Two men, look like brothers, complexion, hair and eyes, very dark; larger one, age about 30; height, five feet, five inches; weight, 145 pounds; may have slight growth of whiskers; smaller one, age about 28; height, five feet, seven inches; weight 135 pounds; sometimes wears moustache.

Any information concerning these bandits should be promptly forwarded to Union Pacific Railroad Company and to the United States Marshal of Wyoming, at Cheyenne.

UNION PACIFIC RAILROAD COMPANY.
PACIFIC EXPRESS COMPANY.

Omaha, Nebraska, June 10th, 1899.

Top left; Reward poster for train robbers, Union Pacific R.R., 1899. This robbery was later attributed to Butch Cassidy's "Wild Bunch" gang. Top right; "Six amateur desperadoes make a bad break and come to grief on the Ft. Wayne Road." Bottom; Five convicts at Sing Sing Prison make an escape by jumping from bridge to freight train below, Hudson River R.R., May 14, 1875.

Top; Train approaching crossfire of competing factions in miners' war, MacDonald Station, Pa., Pan Handle R.R., 1874. Bottom; Train approaching coal mine explosion, Robbins Mines, Ohio, 1881.

13 · TRAIN WRECKS AND DISASTERS

In the years after the Civil War train accidents became, unfortunately, much too common. Passenger train speeds had generally increased from prewar averages of 30 MPH or less to 35-40 MPH. There was a greater flow of traffic in the day, and now much more of it at night as well. Locomotive and car weights increased and the new engines frequently pulled more cars. This put additional strain on an infrastructure of often ill-maintained tracks and roadbeds and bridges of frequently poor construction. As more wrecks occurred, there were greater incidences of subsequent fires caused by the hot coal stoves or the kerosene lamps that provided heating and lighting. The telegraph-dispatch system, helpful in preventing some types of accidents, was also slow in being implemented.

There is no doubt that publications like *Harper's Weekly* and *Frank Leslie's Illustrated Newspaper* thrived on stories of sensational rail accidents. Occasionally both publications would cover the same wreck and furnish competing stories and illustrations of the tragedy. Some crashes became quite famous, finding their way into popular culture and occasionally into song. This reporting did fuel public outrage and calls for action, but real change came only very slowly.

American railways wielded formidable political power and tended to resist change. The speculative style of railroad building, peculiar to America, was much different from what was happening in Europe. Railways there were always built in settled areas, already having a long history of commerce. Such railways usually were better capitalized, and the infrastructure was built more carefully, of better materials, and maintained with an intention of permanence. As a result wrecks were much less frequent there, and Europeans were scandalized by the awful reports from this country.

One famous tragedy was the bridge collapse on the Lake Shore Railroad near Ashtabula, Ohio, on December 29, 1876. An article in the February 3, 1877, issue of *Scientific American* gives the following details.

A violent snowstorm prevailed at the time. The calamity was occasioned by the sudden breaking down of the iron bridge over the creek near Ashtabula station, while the westward bound express train was crossing the structure.

The train consisted of eleven cars, carrying one hundred and seventy-five passengers, and was drawn by the two engines, the *Socrates* and the *Columbia,* the former leading. The train had stopped at all stations between Erie and Ashtabula except three, and at the time of the disaster was running slowly. As the first engine was passing over the bridge, the engineer felt the structure slowly settle down. He was then about two car lengths from the western end. In an instant he opened wide the throttle, the drawbar connecting the two engines snapped in two by the sudden jerk, and the *Socrates* shot ahead, while the *Columbia* fell through the bridge, and turned bottom up. The express, baggage, and passenger cars followed, the sleeping-car swinging over to one side, and a moment later catching fire from the stove.

As the engineer of the *Socrates,* who alone was in a position to see the disaster in all its terrible details, reports, the entire wreck was a mass of flames in two or three minutes. The engineer of the *Columbia* was thrown head first through the window of his cab, and severely but not dangerously injured. Fed by the fierce wind, the fire made swift progress, and so lighted up the ravine that the neighboring people who had heard the fall hastened to the scene. The snow finally ceased falling, and a colder wind whistled through the snowbound ravine. At midnight the fire was smoldering among the ashes and ironwork which it could not burn.

Ashtabula station was about one-fourth of a mile away. Thither the survivors went as soon as possible, assistance for the injured being rendered by the people of the vicinity and those who went to the scene from the depot. By this means the survivors were lodged in various hotels, when a train with the surgeons of the road on board arrived from Cleveland. Early on the following morning men repaired to the wreck, and began the search for the bodies of those who perished.

But with few exceptions they were either wholly destroyed or burned beyond recognition, except by articles of apparel, jewelry, or the contents of their pockets. Over fifty persons lost their lives, and nearly as many more were badly injured. The depth of the ravine and creek, spanned by the bridge, was seventy-five feet, and the cars fell that distance, going through the ice to the bottom.

The bridge was a Howe truss, built entirely of iron, at a cost of seventy-five thousand dollars, and was eleven years old. It was sixty-nine feet above the water, and had an arch one hundred and fifty feet long in the clear, the whole length of the bridge being one hundred and fifty seven feet. It had been tested with six locomotives, and at the time of the disaster it was considered in perfect condition.

Although today's average viewer may find the pictures of this section much the same, each has a somewhat different story to tell. In his book *Train Wrecks: A Pictorial History of Accidents on the Main Line,* Robert C. Reed differentiates a number of different types: derailments, head-on collisions, rear-end collisions, bridge disasters, telescopes, fires, running-gear failures, hot boxes and broken parts, runaways, crossing accidents, and boiler explosions. The historical sequence of the images that follow are a graphic account of some of these types of accidents and their tragic consequences.

By the year 1890 rail travel had become much safer. This was due primarily to a number of improvements, including better coupling devices and braking systems, the replacement of kerosene lighting with electricity, and coal stove heating with steam radiators, reinforcing passenger cars with metal, the introduction of automatic signaling systems, and greatly improving the infrastructure. It is interesting to note that as the century closed, a fad arose where high-speed locomotive collisions were staged and promoted for the popular entertainment of the masses. On April 30, 1900, perhaps the most famous American train wreck occurred. This took place on the Illinois Central Railroad at Vaughan, Mississippi, taking the life of the engineer, Casey Jones.

"The Horrors of Travel," editorial illustration, *Harper's Weekly*, Sept. 23, 1865.

In August 1865, 17 train accidents resulted in 88 fatalities. Scenes from two wrecks: Top; Rescue of passengers after locomotive of one train, rear-ending another, telescopes through the last car, killing 13, near Bridgeport, Conn., Housatonic R.R., Aug. 14. Bottom; Head-on collision takes five lives near Jamaica, N.Y., Long Island R.R., Aug. 28.

Top; New York Lightning Express rear-ended near Lockland, Ohio; Atlantic & Great Western R.R., Nov. 21, 1867. Bottom; Railroad disaster at Mast Hope, Pa.; Erie line, July 14, 1869.

Top; "Death on the Rail," editorial illustration, *Harper's Weekly*, May 10, 1873. Bottom; Passenger cars on Boston Express derail near Springfield, Mass., Mar. 23, 1872.

Top; Scene of railroad disaster, Meadow Brook, R.I., Apr. 1873. Bottom; Derailment, caused by broken wheel, kills 25 people, Prospect Station, Pa., Dec. 24, 1872.

"The Meadow Brook Disaster—Sticking to his post." Artist's depiction of the heroism of the engineer and fireman just prior to the accident, Apr. 1873.

A head-on collision of two freight trains following signal error, Franklin Grove, Ill., Chicago & North Western R.R., Apr. 29, 1874.

Bridge collapse at Ashtabula Creek, Ohio; Lake Shore, R.R., Dec. 29, 1876.

Top; Accident near Jackson, Mich., kills 18 people, mostly immigrants, Michigan Central R.R., Oct. 1879. Bottom; Excursion train disaster at Wallaston Station, Mass., takes 25 lives, Old Colony R.R., Oct. 8, 1878.

Atlantic Express rear-ended by Tarrytown Special; passengers attempting to extinguish flames of wrecked train with snowballs, near Spuyten Duyvil, N.Y., Hudson River R.R., Jan. 13, 1882 [Webster Wagner, developer of the Wagner Palace Cars, was killed in this wreck].

Head-on collision of an excursion train with a freight train kills 19 people near Silver Creek, N.Y.; New York, Chicago & St. Louis ["Nickel Plate"] R.R., Sept. 14, 1886. Top; Extricating the dead and wounded. Bottom; Wreck of the locomotives and freight train.

Train plunge into the White River in Vermont takes 50-60 lives, Vermont Central R.R., Feb. 1887.

Top; Head-on collision at Savage Station, near New Orleans; Illinois Central R.R., June 19, 1891. Bottom; Accident on eastbound Boston & New York Express near New Haven, Conn., New York, New Haven & Hartford R.R., May 1891.

Top; Locomotive after boiler explosion near Blanchester, Ohio., Dec. 24, 1888. Bottom; Locomotive boiler explosion, Wallingford, Conn., New York, New Haven & Hartford R.R., Dec. 19, 1890.

14 · MISCELLANIA

In this section are placed all of those anomalous pictures that, while not fitting well elsewhere, still seemed important to this book, and thus have merited inclusion here. Some, like the page of historical track engravings, or the page of presidential funeral trains, speak for themselves, and really need no more introduction. Two groups of pictures, however—those of the mountain cog railroads and the more visionary railroad projects of Boynton and Chase-Kirchner—have interesting stories that should briefly be presented here.

In the White Mountains of New Hampshire, a popular nineteenth-century tourist area was known as the Switzerland of America. Between 1866 and 1869, Sylvester Marsh supervised the building of a three-mile railroad up to the heights of Mt. Washington, its tallest peak. The road started from an elevation of 2,668 feet and ascended to the Summit House at its top, at an elevation of 6,291 feet. This severely steep climb had a maximum grade of 1,980 feet on one of its three miles, and thus required a new innovation, pioneered by Marsh, to make possible its operation. An article in the August 21, 1875, issue of *Frank Leslie's Illustrated Newspaper* gives the following elaboration:

The road is built in the most substantial manner, of timber interlaced and bolted, resting on the solid rock of the mountain-side. Besides the usual rails, there is a center rail of peculiar construction, to receive the motive power. It consists of two bars of iron, with connecting cross pieces at a distance of every four inches. A center cog wheel on the locomotive plays into this rail, and secures a steady mode of ascent and descent. The driving wheel of the locomotive is geared into a smaller wheel, which connects directly with the crank. Four revolutions of the engine are required to make one of the driving wheel, thus sacrificing speed to power. The engine is not connected to the car, but simply pushes it up the grade. On the return, it allows the car to follow it down at a slow rate of speed.

The original engines on the line had upright boilers and were later replaced by locomotives having horizontal ones. This railroad and its technology served as a model for many similar ones that followed, including the famous Rigi Railroad of Switzerland, completed in the early 1870s, and the later American line, the Manitou & Pike's Peak Railroad, which opened June 1, 1891. Such lines became known as cog railroads.

While *Scientific American* gave many reports of practical railroad innovations over the years, it also had an occasional fascination for the novel and visionary. In its September 7, 1889, issue, the periodical began the first of several reports on the development of the Boynton Bicycle Railroad system. The first locomotive designed by Eben M. Boynton was built at the Portland [locomotive] Company's works at Portland, Maine. It was shipped in 1889 to Gravesend, Long Island, where it began experimental runs on a portion of road formerly owned by the Sea Beach & Coney Island Railroad. The publication's article gives the following description:

The total height of the machine is fifteen feet six inches, and it has a single driving wheel of seven feet nine inches diameter, with double flanges, to ride on a single rail. The cab is two stories high, the upper story being operated by the engineer, and the lower story by the fireman. . . . The passenger cars to be drawn by this engine are to be four feet wide and fourteen feet high, in two stories, forty feet long, weigh five tons, and designed to carry one hundred eight passengers. The engine and train are to be kept on their single track by upper wooden guiding beams supported fifteen feet above the track by a bridge-like skeleton frame arching over the roadway.

The system was designed so that two Boynton trains could run in opposite directions on a typical standard gauge line, one train on each rail without touching the other. It was intended in this system to greatly reduce both weight and friction, thus saving power and reducing cost.

A follow-up article in the *Scientific American* of March 28, 1891, reported some progress: a new engine had been built and for some weeks the previous summer had carried passengers between Gravesend and Coney Island. Besides having an engraving of this train, the article also included one showing a proposed train, with an improved engine, designed for a street railway using the Boynton system. It appears that shortly afterward the Boynton Company turned its attention from steam to electrical power. The magazine's February 17, 1894, issue gives the updated account:

The need of the day is rapid transit. Steam, cable, and trolley cars each in their own degree contribute to this end. The accompanying illustrations show one of the last developments in true rapid transit—the Boynton Electric Bicycle Railroad—of which a line is now in the process of erection across Long Island, from Bellport to the Sound. The idea of the bicycle railroad is to provide a system of transit whose speed may be from seventy-five to one hundred or more m.p.h. Air resistance being one of the most adverse factors at this velocity, a car of small cross sectional area is preferable. The inequalities of two parallel lines of rail is also a factor of resistance. In the railroad in question a narrow car with sharpened ends is employed, and is mounted upon two wheels, one at each end, and travels upon a single rail. It has the equilibrium of the bicycle, and like the latter disposes at once of the violent transverse wrenching strains which affect four wheeled vehicles of the everyday type. It is peculiarly well adapted for electric propulsion, the overhead rail giving a place for the current main.

It is doubtful that this railroad made much more progress, yet it incorporated some good ideas and did meet with limited success. The Chase-Kirchner Railroad proposal, reported in the May 5, 1894, issue of *Scientific American,* probably remained only a dream, despite its having some daring and innovative ideas. The primary idea of this system was to wed wind power with electrical power in an attempt to create trains capable of speeds of 125 to 150 MPH. The system required a straight-line roadway, however, allowing no curves, although it could go up or down elevations with no problem. It was not ideally suited for short distances, but was proposed for possible transcontinental use. It is interesting that the dreamers of that time actually anticipated trains of the kind operating in Europe and Japan today, ones easily attaining such speeds, but with far superior modern technology.

Locomotive stopped by pedestrian traffic on Pennsylvania Ave. after adjournment of Congress, Washington D.C., April 1866.

Top; President Garfield's funeral train, Princeton, N.J., Camden & Amboy R.R., Oct. 1881. Bottom; President Grant's funeral train, West Point, N.Y., New York, West Shore & Buffalo R.R., July 1885.

Historical exhibit of rails at the Columbian Exposition, Chicago, 1893.

Cog railroads: View of rail line and Summit House, Mt. Washington R.R., White Mountains, N.H., 1875.

Cog railroads: Train on trestle in scenic New Hampshire, Mt. Washington R.R., 1879.

Cog railroads: Train ascending grade up to Pike's Peak, Colo., elevation 14,110 ft., Manitou & Pike's Peak R.R., 1891.

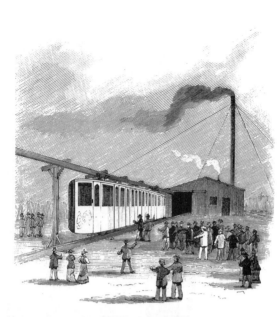

Visionary railroads: Top left; The original Boynton Bicycle Locomotive, 1889. Top right; Station near Patchogue, L.I., Boynton Bicycle Elevated Railroad, 1894.
Middle; Boynton design for improved locomotive for street railway use, 1891. Bottom; Boynton experimental single rail train in operation at Gravesend, L.I., 1890-91.

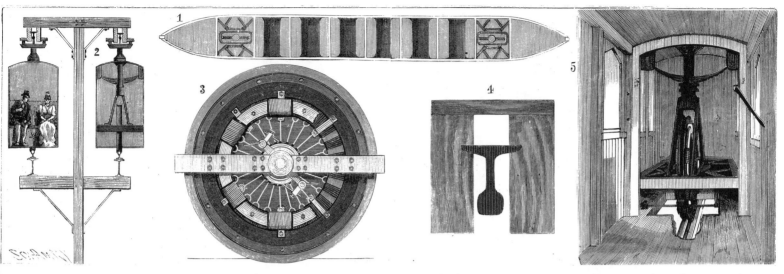

Visionary railroads: Top; Details of track, motor and car construction: The Boynton Bicycle Elevated Railroad, 1894. Bottom: Artist's depiction of the improved Boynton Bicycle Elevated Railroad, 1894.

Visionary railroads: The Chase-Kirchner Aerodromic Railroad, 1894. Top left; Bird's-eye view. Top right; Cross-section of car and track support apparatus. Bottom; View of car and passenger platform.

15 · HORSE RAILWAYS

In the 1820s horse-drawn omnibuses began appearing in American cities. Unlike the small hack cabs that were hired for any destination, these began operating over certain routes, dropping and taking on passengers. Essentially stagecoaches adapted for city use, they soon were redesigned and built for carrying more passengers. More economical than hacks, they filled a previously unrecognized public need and quickly became popular.

As small intercity horse-drawn railroads began operation in the late 1820s, some saw the possibility of this technology being adapted for urban omnibus use. In November 1832 John Mason inaugurated a horse-drawn line in Manhattan that began on Prince Street and ran to Fourteenth Street. He had two cars built by John Stephenson, a young manufacturer of coaches and omnibuses. The first car, named for Mason, was essentially a stagecoach designed for rails and carrying thirty passengers. Later cars became more influenced by omnibus design. Mason's company eventually evolved into the New York & Harlem Railroad, which later ran steam trains from 26th Street north to Harlem, while continuing its horsecar operation in lower Manhattan.

In 1834 a line was built in New Orleans that ran on Magazine Street. There was an early resistance to this new mode of transportation in many places, but in the 1850s it became increasingly popular. By then, lines had spread over much of Manhattan and Brooklyn. In 1856 lines were opened in Boston and Cambridge. In 1858 streetcars began operation in Philadelphia, and in 1859 they were running in Chicago, Pittsburgh, and Cincinnati. Within a short time they were operating in much smaller towns as well.

Although limited to the lines over which they operated, streetcars had the advantage over omnibuses in comfort and carrying capacity. They typically had a speed over their routes of about six miles an hour. After completing a run, they were turned around, usually on a small turntable, and returned to their point of origin. Later some cars were designed in a way where the carriage body itself could be swiveled around the other way, thus simplifying the procedure. Originally drivers received the fares, but as this became increasingly awkward, conductors were employed to take them. Drivers and conductors had long shifts, typically twelve or even sixteen hours for six days a week.

Bad weather was difficult for streetcars. In the early years hay was often strewn on the floor when it was cold. Later small coal stoves were used, but these would usually overheat those closest to them. Other heating devices were tried, but nothing proved too effective. Packed snow could easily derail a street car. Snowplows and rock salt were used with some success, but cleared tracks were an obstacle to those traveling in sleighs, so for years their use was prohibited in some cities. Lines occasionally tried pulling large sleighs along their routes in winter, but this never became general practice.

Beginning in the 1860s, new designs began appearing on streetcars. The driver's position was moved from a high perch to a front platform. The bobtail car, a somewhat truncated design pulled by a single horse, began operation in New Orleans in 1865. It was intended for use in areas of low passenger volume. The monitor roof, a split-level design adapted from railroad passenger cars, was introduced in 1873. It provided the advantage of better lighting and ventilation. The carmaker John Stephenson went on to become the largest manufacturer of streetcars in the world, exporting his superior products to many different countries.

Unlike drivers and conductors, horses were worked for only a few hours each day. Typically, companies might have five to ten horses for each car they owned; thus their investment in animals was substantial. They owned stables, employing farriers, hostlers, veterinarians, managers, and other individuals as needed. Although horses did have to suffer the burden of overloaded cars and hot summers, reports of driver cruelty were perhaps overly sensationalized by the media.

Horse teams typically pulled a car for about fifteen miles and were retired for the day. A horse pulling a bobtail might be replaced after ten miles. Horses were usually sold when they might still be useful for a few more years. Mules were used by some lines, but were more difficult to sell at retirement. The sale of manure brought additional revenues for the companies. In late 1872, a severe epidemic of equine influenza killed many thousands of horses used by the lines, temporarily incapacitating their operations.

In his book *Trolley Car Treasury,* Frank Rowsome states that by 1886 there were 525 horsecar lines in three hundred cities and towns, employing one hundred thousand animals. He also writes:

> Cars had also begun to specialize. Plush extra-fare parlor cars for refined passengers appeared. There were genteel cars for ladies only, safe from the annoyances of coarse language and tobacco smoke. Double-decker cars were tried out on high-traffic runs. Special horsecars carried mail, mixed freight, sheep, chickens, and sand or gravel. Horsecars could be rented for weddings and outings, as could black-curtained horsecar hearses.

Horsecar lines reached their zenith in 1888. While able to coexist with cable cars, they fell victim to the rapid development of the faster electric trolley car. By the turn of the century, horsecar lines were largely gone, but they continued in a few places until about the time of the First World War.

Mules drawing freight cars on street line, Dock St., Philadelphia, 1854 [Omnibus depot and Philadelphia Exchange in background].

BELLEW

Top; Street railway in New Orleans, double-decker car, 1855. Bottom; The Cambridge & Boston Horse R.R. in Bowdoin Square, Mass., 1856.

Top; Pulling stalled car in front of the Tombs, Centre St., Manhattan; New York & Harlem R.R., 1857. Bottom; Metropolitan R.R. snowplow operating in the "neck," Boston, 1857.

Top; Opening of the Baltimore City R.R., July 20, 1859. Bottom; Horse cars racing on the Bowery, New York, 1865.

Horse cars attempting to operate in a blizzard, New York, Jan. 17, 1867.

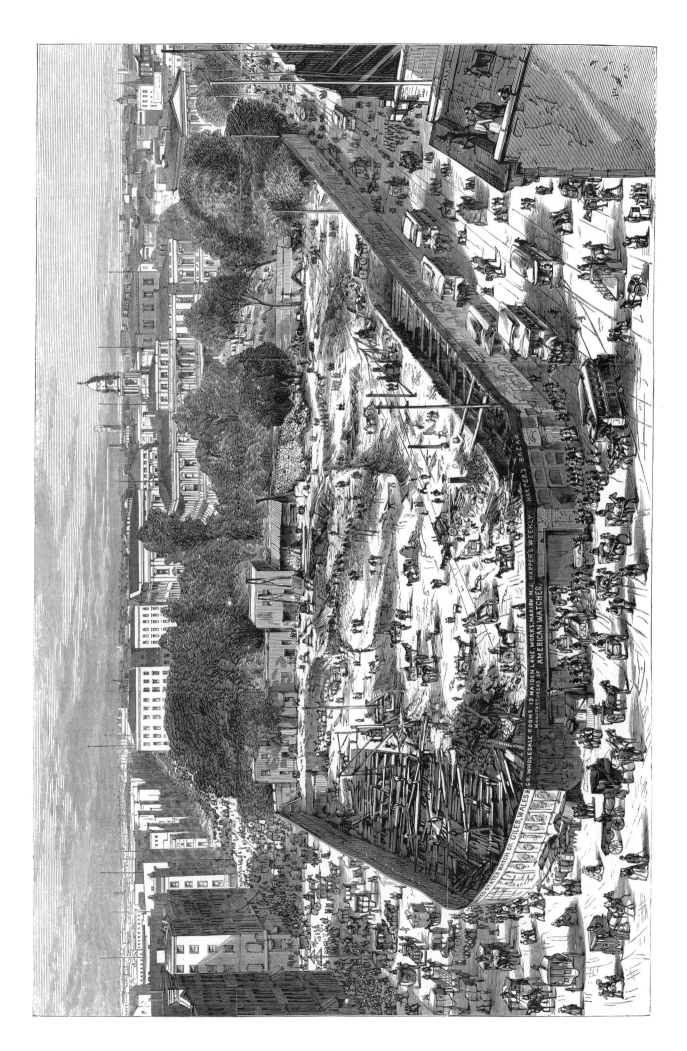

Horse cars and other street traffic at construction site near City Hall, New York, 1869.

Top left; Depot for 3rd Ave. Street Ry., New York, c.1872. Top right; Car drawn by two horses, c.1870. Middle left; Original horse car built by Stephenson, New York, 1832. Middle right; Portable horse railway, c.1872. Bottom; Snowplow for horse cars, 1868.

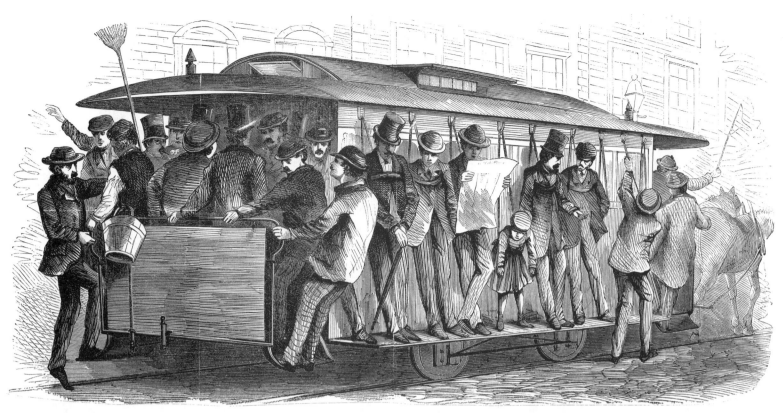

Top; Overcrowded street car, New York, 1867. Bottom; Overcrowded car, tired horses being checked, New York, 1872.

Top left; Mules receive rest as car descends grade in San Bernadino, County, Calif., Ontario & San Antonio Heights R.R., 1880s. Top right; Palace car, 3rd Ave. street car line, New York, 1871. Upper middle left; "Bob-tail" style car, Lindell Railway Co., St. Louis, c.1870. Lower middle left; Street car, New Orleans, c.1870. Bottom left; Car of Union Passenger Railway Co., Philadelphia, c.1870. Bottom right; Improved fare box, c.1872.

Top; Cars blockaded by snow in the Bowery, New York, 1871. Bottom; "Beauties of street car travel in New York," editorial illustration, *Harper's Weekly*, May 20, 1871.

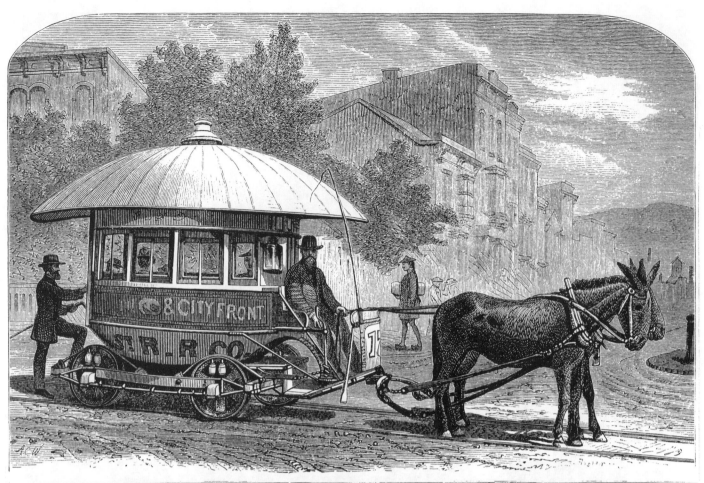

Top; Balloon swivel car, Market St. Ry., San Francisco, 1872. Bottom; Horse car accident near Bergen Hill, N.J., 1876.

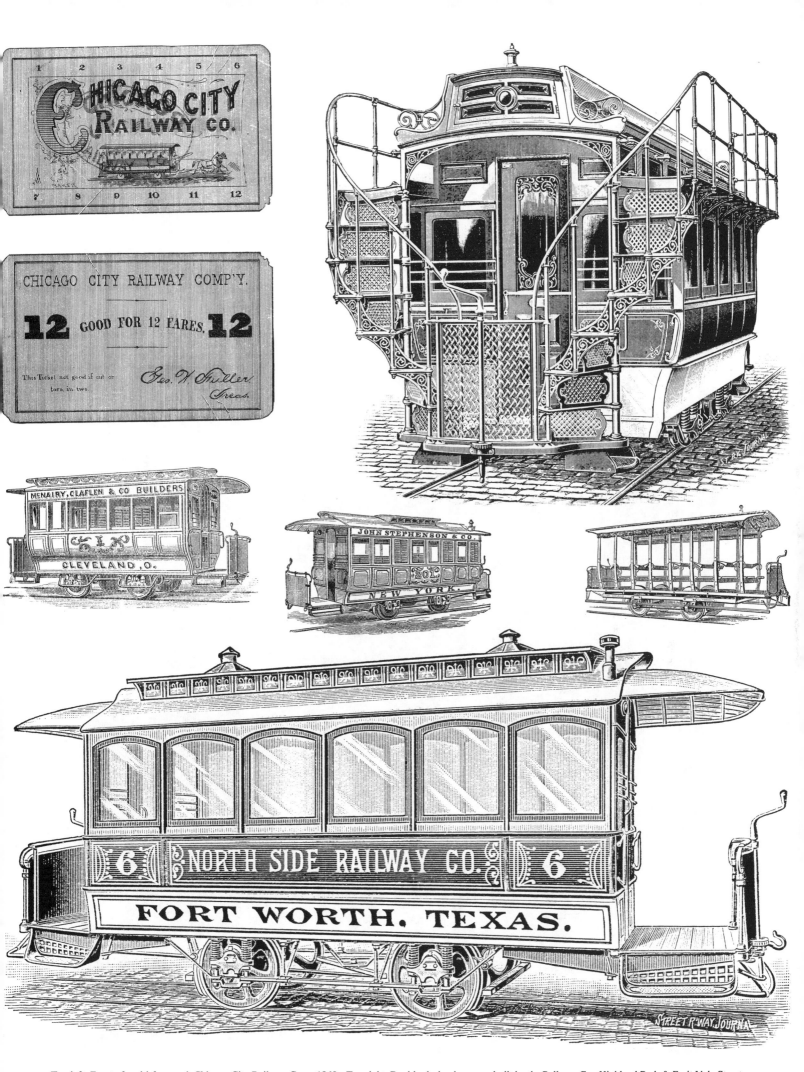

Top left; Front of multi-fare card, Chicago City Railway Co., c.1860s. Top right; Double-decker horse car built by the Pullman Co., Highland Park & Fruit Vale Street Ry., Oakland, Calif., 1891. Upper middle left; Back side of multi-fare card. Middle left; Car of McNairy, Claflen & Co., c.1872. Middle center; Car of John Stephenson & Co., c.1870. Middle right; Open car for summer use, c.1879. Bottom; Horse car built by the Calumet Car Co., Chicago, c.1889.

"The car driver's Christmas dinner," 1878.

Strike of conductors and drivers, West Division Street Ry., Chicago, 1885.

Horses stopped to water, 3rd Ave. Street Ry., New York, July 1890.

One of the greatest weaknesses of horsecar lines was their vulnerability when operated up steep inclines. In 1869, Andrew Smith Hallidie, a manufacturer of wire cable in San Francisco, witnessed an accident of a type all too frequent in that city. A team of four horses pulling a car up a hill stalled, and when one horse slipped, the car dragged the horses back down the hill for some distance, severely injuring them and requiring their disposal. Hallidie, familiar with ways mining companies used cables for moving ore, became resolved to employ similar techniques and design a practical cable-car system.

The system that he designed required a long underground housing beneath the streets, in which an endlessly moving cable, drawn by a stationary steam engine, might function. The driver, called the gripman, would operate a device that extended below the car through a slot in the street and engaged the cable. When stopping the car, the cable would be released and brakes employed. In his excavations for a line on Clay Street, Hallidie's progress was continually delayed by gas, water, and sewer lines that had to be relocated.

The Clay Street line began experimental operation on August 1, 1873, and soon it had an average net income of three thousand dollars a month. Five or six other lines soon began construction in San Francisco. In April 1878, the California Street line opened with much fanfare and highly decorated cars. By 1883 there were lines in Brooklyn, Hoboken, Chicago, St. Louis, Kansas City, Omaha, Los Angeles, and Oakland. At its maximum point, the St. Louis system had fifty-five miles of track. Chicago's system, begun in 1882, became the largest in the world. Later New York, Washington, D.C., and Philadelphia all built large systems as well.

From the beginning, the public was concerned about the strength and durability of cables, whether or not they might break. It became the custom to inspect the cables each night, following the close of service. Although cables usually were only one and a quarter to two inches thick, they were extremely well made and generally would last about seventy-five thousand miles—about a year of normal operation. Cables typically might be three to four miles long, but one in Denver was seven miles in length. On rare occasions, when one or two strands on a cable might break, a grip could become stuck, thus leaving the car impossible to stop. In *Trolley Car Treasury,* Frank Rowsome gives the following description:

When the gripman found himself unable to pull free by hard braking, he would jangle his gong in loud, continuous warning. Before long he would catch up with the car ahead, perhaps letting off or loading passengers. Its gripman, hearing the desperate alarm signal behind, would instantly start up to avoid a collision and begin clanging his gong too. Sometimes, according to cable folklore, as many as five or six cars would go clanging along the street, urgently fleeing the runaway at the end of the procession.

Besides having the advantage of operating better on grades, cable cars had other advantages over horsecars. They were faster, typically going 8 to 9 MPH, smoother, free from stable odors and unseemly horse defecations, relatively noiseless, and could operate better in the cold, in snow, and with heavy loads. They had the advantage over steam cars of being unlikely to give off gases, catch fire, or explode.

Cable lines did have problems with their slots, which expanded on hot days and contracted on cold ones. An opened slot might capture a narrow buggy wheel or otherwise plague the unwary. Juvenile pranksters liked to attach things to the cables, thus creating raucous noises, or cleverly devise other torments to sabotage the lines. Cables had a tendency to expand during the course of their lifetimes. "Dead spots" existed where cars made turns, sometimes requiring passengers to assist in pushing the car to a point where the cable could again be engaged.

Furthermore, cable-car lines were so expensive to build that their construction was limited largely to areas of high-volume traffic, or where elevations were too difficult for horsecars. Once the lines were built, however, operating costs were much lower than for horsecar lines. Cable lines continued to expand until about 1890, at which time there were about five thousand cars operating on five hundred miles of track, and serving 400 million passengers annually. By 1895, cable lines were rapidly being dismantled in favor of trolleys. Philadelphia and Providence changed over that year, and Baltimore in 1897. The systems in St. Louis and Chicago barely survived the turn of the century. Cable cars live on today only in the city of their origin, San Francisco.

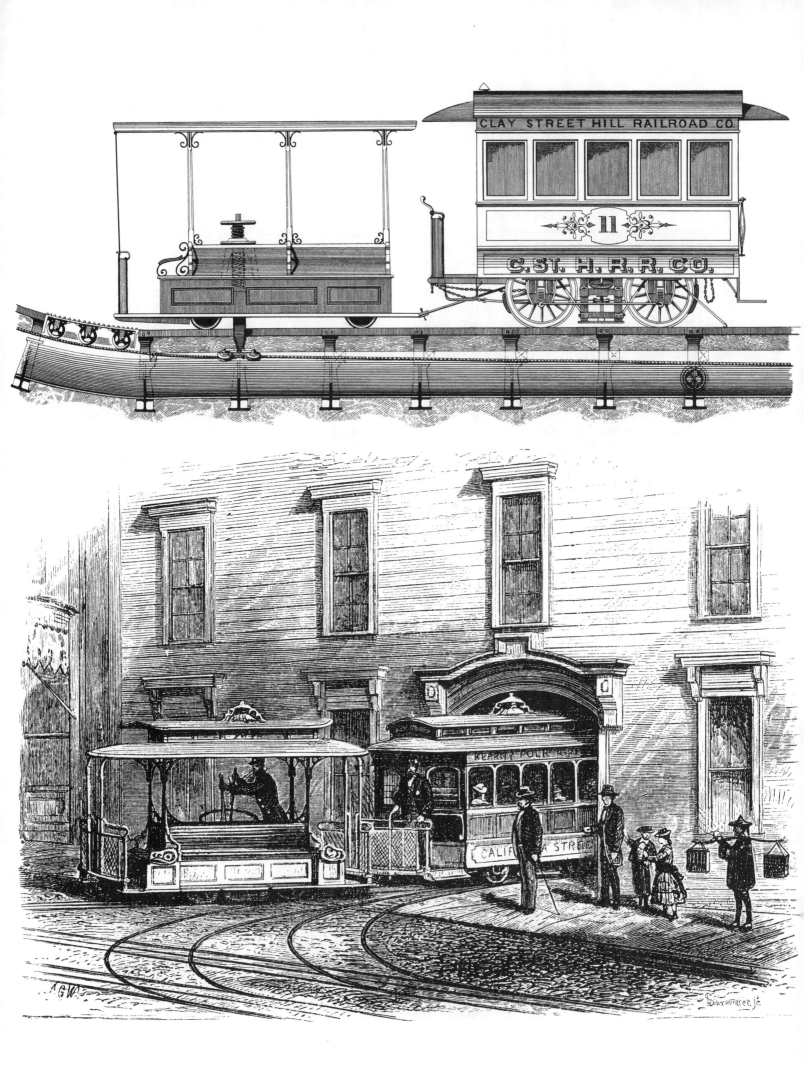

Top; The first cable system in San Francisco; grip car and street car with cut-away view of cable underneath, Clay St. Hill R.R., c.1873. Bottom; Leaving the car house, California Street R.R. Co., San Francisco, 1878.

Top; Hoboken inclined cable railway, Hoboken, N.J., 1886. Bottom; Cable railroad in operation; grip car drawing street car, California Street R.R. Co., 1878.

Laying of Broadway Cable R.R., near Union Square, New York, 1891.

A gripman in winter, Chicago, 1893.

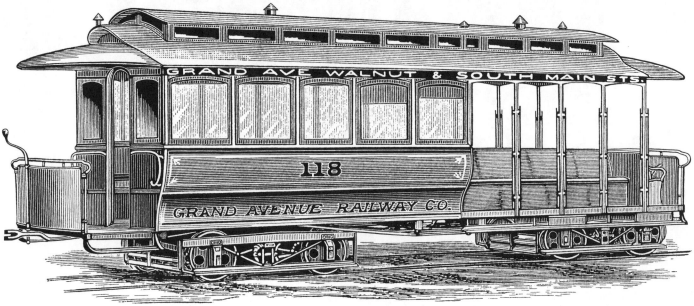

Top; Underground cable pulleys opposite the Houston St. power house, Broadway Cable Railway, New York, 1893. Bottom; Combination grip and passenger "California" style cable car, Grand Avenue Railway Co., Kansas City, Mo., c.1890.

A GREAT CLUTCH & PULLEY

THE ROPE BELT

THE GRIP

SCIENTIFIC AMERICAN N.Y.

POWER HOUSE INTERIOR

ONE OF THE GREAT CORLISS ENGINES

BOWERY & 23 3D AVENUE

CITY HALL TO CENTRAL PARK & HARLEM BRIDGE

THIRD AVE 23

THE NEW CABLE CAR

GRIP & BREAK LEVERS

New cable traction plant and other views of operation, Third Avenue Cable Railway, New York, 1894.

17 · STEAM CARS AND ELECTRIC TROLLEYS

somewhat neglected aspect of railroad history has been the importance of the inventors. Though early developers of the steam locomotive like Trevithick and Stephenson remain in our memories, the names of many others, both early tinkerers and later contributors, do not. The story of the transition from the horse-drawn streetcar through experimental phases to the electrified trolley is, much like the story of the locomotive, strewn with the wreckage of discarded ideas. Eccentric and, occasionally, visionary individuals wrestled with seemingly insurmountable problems and sometimes even solved them. Perhaps the zeitgeist of the nineteenth century was truly one of invention, where people working in many areas made slow, yet still amazing, progress.

In hopes of finding a technology that would revolutionize streetcar transportation, inventors tried many things. The successful development of the steam locomotive led to expectations that steam could also be adapted for powering streetcars. Later, especially in the 1870s and 1880s, ammonia gas, naphtha, giant clock springs, compressed air, and other potential power sources were experimented with as well, but soon discarded as impractical.

The earliest steam car appears to have been invented for a Cincinnati streetcar line in 1859 by A. B. Latta. It was reputed to carry eighty passengers. Soon thereafter, Grice & Long of Philadelphia constructed a long steam car, with two trucks. Steam power was applied to one of the trucks by means of a toothed gear. By 1860, five to six steam cars of rather primitive design were in operation in the United States. Some were tried on regular rail lines to handle commuter and short-distance passenger traffic.

Following the Civil War, primitive steam cars were tried in New York on the Second Avenue line. Heavier track had to be laid, but service became faster and, so it seemed for a while, less costly. The experiment ultimately proved a failure, however, when the steam engines all began wearing out at once. The replacement costs proved too excessive, and horses were soon returned to the line. Despite this failure, a few steam cars were manufactured in Trenton, New Jersey, before 1870, and Baldwin introduced its own production in 1873. In 1876 steam cars began service on Philadelphia's Market Street line.

Besides requiring heavier track and being costly, steam cars had other problems. They were noisy and dirty, expelling excessive amounts of smoke and soot into the air, and were frightening to horses. Human passengers, with some justification, were also uneasy about them, for fear of a boiler explosion. Later, attempts were made to disguise steam cars in a way that made them less frightening to horses. Dummies—small locomotives having vertical boilers and masquerading as street cars—were sometimes used, pulling one or two real cars behind them.

One interesting and inventive attempt to solve these problems was the development of the "fireless" steam engine. In 1872, after failing in attempts to power a streetcar with ammonia gas, Dr. Emile Lamm built a small experimental locomotive that began pulling streetcars on the Crescent City Railroad, a six-mile line between New Orleans and Carrolton. His guiding principle was that if water is heated in a pressure-resistant container with no space for it to expand and become steam, it will remain liquid and build up heat and pressure. If a device could be opened to bleed off the superpressurized water, it would spontaneously become steam and drive the engine. Lamm's locomotive contained a large reservoir of water. Before each trip, the reservoir would be filled with cold water and connected to the steam pipe of a stationary boiler. The water would heat rapidly to a high pressure, and the steam pipe would be disconnected. His locomotive could go a distance of approximately twelve miles before its power was exhausted. The Crescent City line was still operating a number of these locomotives in 1877. Nonetheless, the fireless engine did not catch on elsewhere in this country, perhaps because of its distance limitations.

Although various steam vehicles were operated on street or commuter lines in a number of cities, the technology never became refined or practical enough for widespread adoption. It remained to the electric trolley to provide this badly needed breakthrough.

This technology took quite a while to develop. In 1834, Thomas Davenport, a blacksmith who had become fascinated by magnets, built the first small electric motor. In 1839 a Scotsman, Robert Davidson, created an electric locomotive powered by a primitive battery. It achieved a speed of 4 MPH but was destroyed one night by some rowdy railroad employees, and never rebuilt.

In 1850, the U.S. Congress provided funds for Professor Charles G. Page to build an electric locomotive, which was to be run on a four-and-a-half-mile track from Washington to Bladensburg, Maryland. His rather ungainly locomotive made its debut April 29, 1851, performing rather spasmodically but still completing its journey in thirty-nine minutes. Unfortunately, the return took much longer, as the battery cells began rapidly failing. Several ingenious rewirings by Page managed to get the locomotive back home, but this did not save it from the congressional ax.

A Belgian, Zenobie Theophile Gramme, builder of the first successful dynamo in 1870, discovered by 1872 that this generator could also function as a motor. Adapting this discovery, Wemer Siemens, a German, displayed a small electric locomotive at the Berlin Industrial Exhibition of 1879. In 1881 Siemens inaugurated a small electric street line using a converted horsecar. This car used a simple two-rail system, receiving current from one rail and releasing it to the other. It had some success, but people complained of shocks when crossing the line, and short circuits occurred in rainy weather.

At Menlo Park, New Jersey, in 1880, Thomas Edison constructed a dynamo-driven locomotive and began experiments with it. Although impressive speeds were reached, and the locomotive upgraded a few times, it never gained much attention from Edison, and the project was finally dropped.

Other inventors were also trying to come up with a workable system. In 1883, Leo Daft built the *Ampere*, a two-ton locomotive with a 25-horsepower motor, which used a third-rail system. Following this, Daft quickly built two more locomotives. One, which was being operated at Coney Island for the amusement of visitors, impressed an official of a Baltimore street line. This official, Thomas Robbins, made it possible for Daft to experiment on a three-mile line there that had hilly terrain. For this, Daft built three small locomotives, hooking each to a horsecar. A successful trial was made August 9, 1885, and the line opened for service the next day. Soon speed on the line was greatly improved, doubling that of horses. However, his third-rail system proved vulnerable in the rain, with people receiving shocks and small animals occasionally being electrocuted. The line ran for over a year but was finally returned to the horses.

By the late 1880s, Daft had found a new system. Installing an electric motor underneath a horsecar, he connected this by wire to two poles that extended up from the roof. Each pole had a grooved-wheel "troller" at its end, which rolled on a live wire suspended overhead and received current. This innovation solved Daft's previous problems, but a new one developed: the trollers constantly fell off the wires, disrupting service on each occasion. Despite this drawback, Daft System Trolleys soon began operation in Asbury Park and Orange, New Jersey, and a few other cities. One of Daft's competitors was Charles J. Van Depoele, a Belgian-American, who in the early 1880s also experimented with an overhead troller system. Unlike Daft's, this one pressed up against the wire, with the troller running underneath.

In 1885, at the Toronto Exposition, Van Depoele provided an electric locomotive pulling three cars that ferried visitors from the railroad station to the exposition grounds, a distance of about a mile. During one five-day period it carried fifty thousand passengers. Soon Van Depoele adapted his system for streetcars and built lines in South Bend, Indiana, Scranton, Pennsylvania, and a few other cities. Unlike Daft, he located the motor of his cars on the front platform, next to the motorman. The weight of the motors was too heavy, and soon the platforms began to shake loose.

The individual who finally emerged to perfect the electrical trolley system was Frank Sprague. A true genius, Sprague was born in Connecticut in 1857. Trained in mathematics and engineering, he graduated from Annapolis with high honors and received a commission in the navy. Upon resigning his commission, Sprague took employment with Thomas Edison, but stayed less than a year. His academic style contrasted sharply with that of Edison and his assistants, who were all self-taught. Still, Sprague found shortcuts to some of the Edison technical procedures and thus gained respect. He saw the experimental locomotive there but found it unimpressive. In his spare time, Sprague began a working model for a railway motor.

In the spring of 1884 he formed the Sprague Electric Railway and Motor Company. His motors, for the first time ever, were designed as motors, rather than adapted dynamos. Soon after they were exhibited at the Philadelphia Exposition of 1884, he began receiving orders from Europe as well as America. Sprague started experimenting with installing two-gear-driven electric motors in a single railroad truck. They were mounted in such a way as to absorb bumps and still function. He also developed the idea of regenerative braking, where the motors temporarily become generators while braking, thus slowing the car down, and generating a little electricity as well. He successfully staged a demonstration of this system on the Manhattan Elevated.

In May 1887 Sprague began the building of a complete electrical railway in Richmond, Virginia, which would have twelve miles of track. Many problems plagued his efforts, but by February 2, 1888, the line opened service. Overcoming still other problems, the line was running relatively smooth by summer and attracted national attention. Soon Sprague sold his system to a horsecar line in Boston. By the end of the decade two hundred trolley lines were either under construction or already in service—90 percent operating under Sprague's patents.

In 1889 Sprague's company was absorbed by Edison's. Afterwards he continued to work independently, making many other contributions, and maintained efforts until his death in 1934. Trolleys were to gain maximum popularity in the first two decades of this century. Today, in cities like San Francisco, Philadelphia, and New Orleans, a few lines are still preserved.

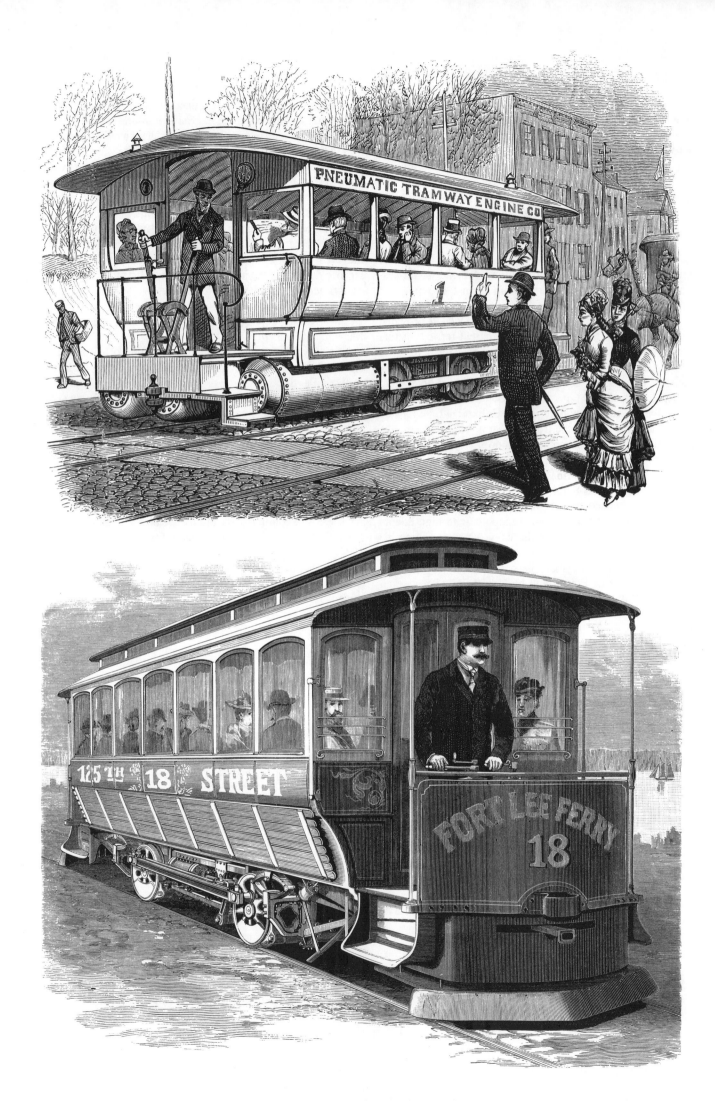

Top; Trial trip of a pneumatic car on the 2nd Ave. street car line, New York, 1878. Bottom; Trial of the Hardie Compressed Air Car, New York, 1896.

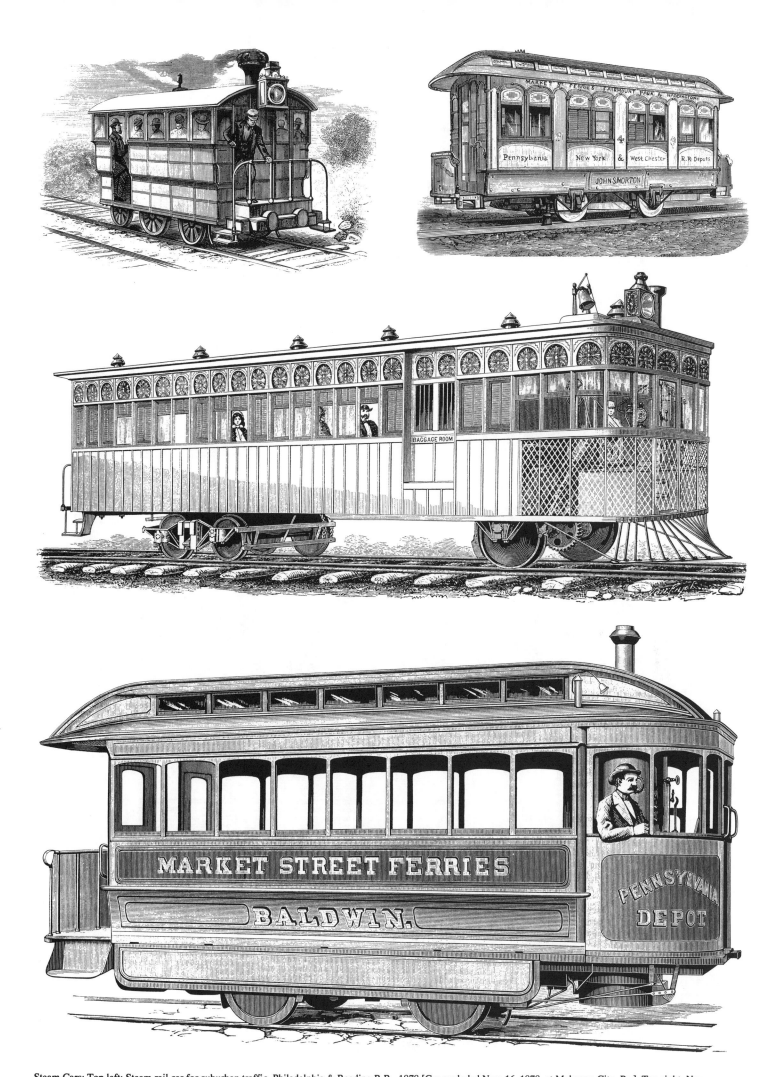

Steam Cars: Top left; Steam rail car for suburban traffic, Philadelphia & Reading R.R., 1878 [Car exploded Nov. 16, 1878, at Mahanoy City, Pa.]. Top right; New steam street car for Market Street line, Philadelphia, 1877. Middle; Steam rail car, Grice and Long Co., 1861. Bottom; Baldwin steam powered street car, Market Street line, Philadelphia, 1876.

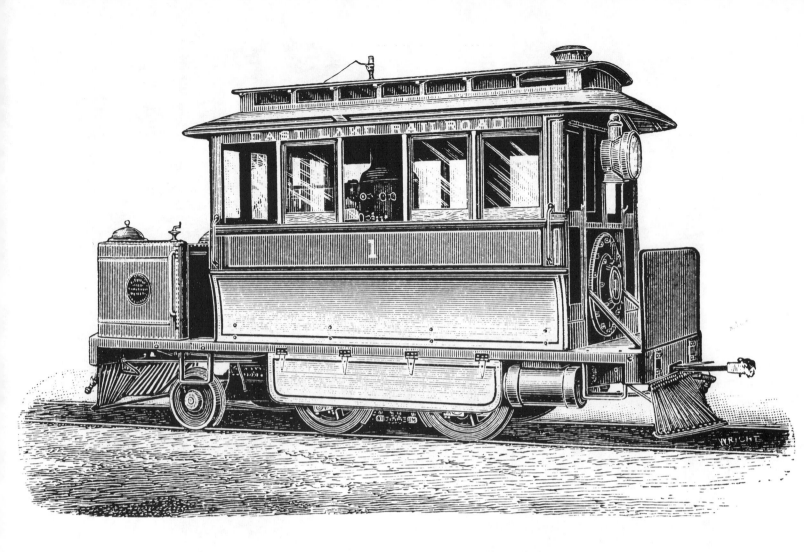

Steam "dummy" locomotives for drawing street cars: Top; Baldwin, c.1888. Bottom; Porter, 1893.

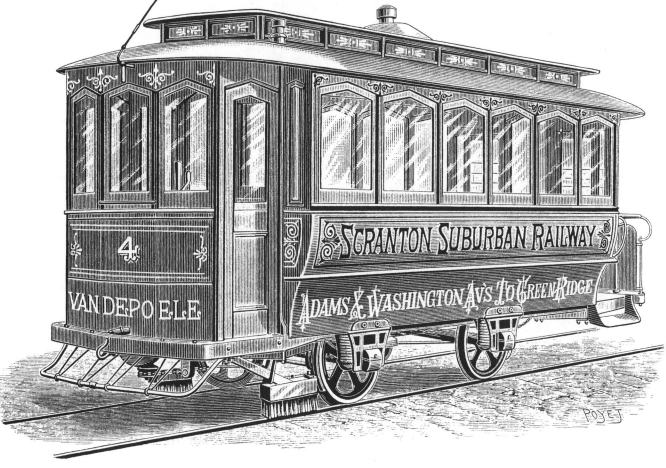

Top; Edison's second experimental electric locomotive, Menlo Park, N.J., 1882. Bottom; Van Depoele system trolley, Scranton Suburban Ry., 1887.

Trolley cars, c.1891. Top left; Single-truck trolley, Brooklyn. Top right; Trolley of West End Street Ry., Boston. Upper middle left; Single-truck trolley, Utica, N.Y. Lower middle; Double-truck open trolley for summer use, Lowell & Dracut Street Ry. Bottom; Double-truck trolley, Lindell Ry., St. Louis.

Combined Electric Snow Sweeper, General Electric Co., 1892.

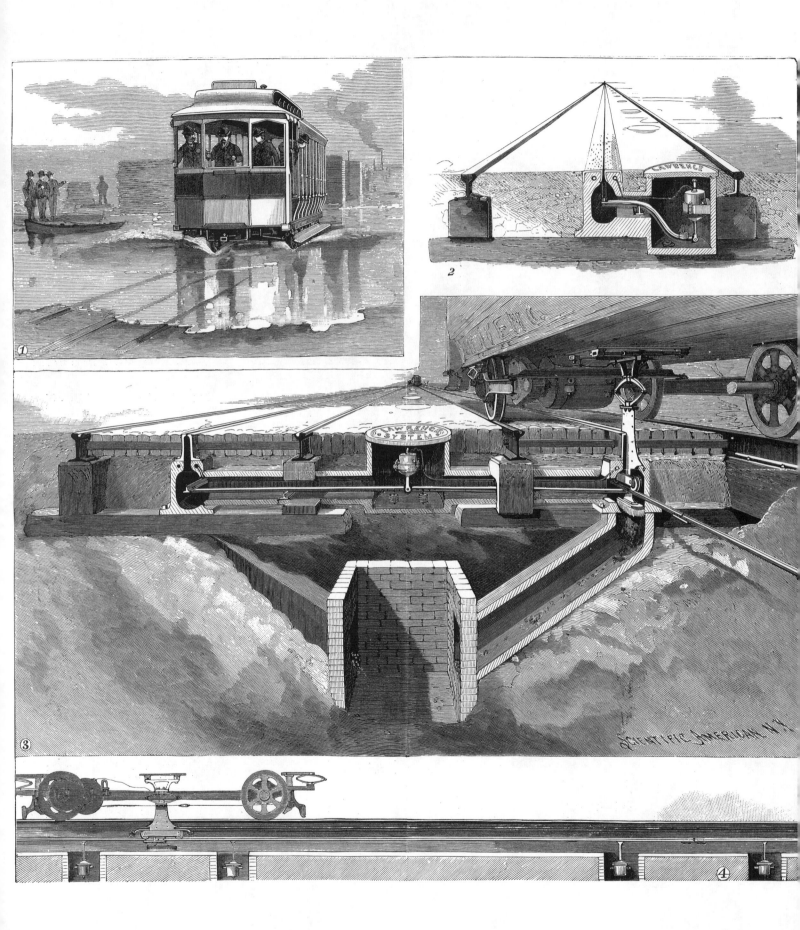

Lawrence underground conduit electric railroad, 1894.

Although the adoption of horsecar street lines in New York had initially made some improvement in transportation there, the continued rapid growth of population, commerce, and port traffic, squeezed into the city's narrow confines, eventually created a problem of immense magnitude; one unique to this country. Beginning about 1853, *Scientific American,* shortly followed by other periodicals, began occasionally to feature illustrated articles about various proposed solutions to this problem. An illustrated article on a proposed plan by James H. Swett in the November 5, 1853, issue of *Frank Leslie's Illustrated Newspaper* offered the following observation:

> Citizens of almost every city have projected plans to relieve New York Broadway of its bustle below, by endeavoring to elevate some of it above. No one who has anxiously waited for twenty minutes to cross Broadway in order to reach our office, and that at the evident risk of a collision with an omnibus, but has offered up a petition for some relief for that over-crowded thoroughfare. No city in the world, we believe, has such an overcrowded street as Broadway, below the Park, with vehicles of every description. To remedy the evil, various plans have been proposed, but none have come so near being carried out as a railway in the middle of the street, the grant for which was given by our immaculate Aldermen, but averted by a legal injunction. Many, however, contend that no ground railway can afford relief to Broadway, hence ways have been devised to spread the travel, to divide the people, by allowing some to be traveling above, while others are traveling below.

Swett's plan was for an elevated rail system employing steam locomotives for drawing cars. Many other plans were offered in the following years: elevated horsecar lines; elevated cars pulled by rope or cable systems; elaborately designed elevated roads where the whole street below was covered in shadow; pneumatic-powered elevated or subway systems; steam-powered subway railroads, and more. Although a subway system was developed in London in the 1860s and seemed most ideal for New York, the construction costs would have been too great for the city. Finally, in 1867, the inventor Charles T. Harvey began construction of the world's first elevated railway on Greenwich Street, originally employing a cable to draw the cars. By July 1868 the line extended from the Battery to Dey Street and the cars could reach speeds of about 15 MPH. This line, originally incorporated as the New York Elevated Railroad, became the New York Elevated Railroad Company in 1870, when the original company was sold after it was determined that the cable system was a failure. The new company tried an 0-4-0 dummy engine on the line and this proved to work much better. By then the line had already been extended up Greenwich Street, and then 9th Avenue, to reach 30th Street. By 1876 it ran to 59th Street.

Wind power was used in the experimental Broadway Pneumatic Underground Railroad, which operated between Warren and Murray streets underneath Broadway. Invented by A. E. Beach, it opened in 1870 and lasted until 1873. Up to twenty-two passengers would board the car on a slight grade. The operator would then release the brake and the car would descend past the wind tunnel, then be propelled at about 6 MPH onto its destination. It probably was more of a curiosity for sightseers and tourists than anything else. The city had no interest in Beach's system, which finally went out of business. However, Dr. Rufus H. Gilbert, who soon would become the dominant figure of elevated lines in the city, for a time favored this technology.

Dr. Gilbert, the son of an associate judge in Steuben County, had studied mechanics before embarking on a career in medicine. Following the death of his wife, he dropped his medical practice and traveled to London and Paris to study the hospital systems there. While there he became interested in public-health issues, observing the plight of the poor living in crowded tenement houses. He came to the conclusion that another remedy was needed besides that of medicine. To give them a better chance to live, they must have better accommodations and purer air, and the key to solving this problem lay in providing rapid transit—allowing them to live further from their place of work.

Dr. Gilbert returned to America on the eve of the Civil War and immediately enlisted in a Zouave regiment as a surgeon. His service was distinguished and he rose to the position of medical director and superintendent of the U.S. Army Hospitals. Suffering from ill health following the war, he dropped the medical profession and took a position as assistant to the superintendent of the Central Railroad of New Jersey. Here he had time to study thoroughly the problem of rapid transit. He resigned his position in 1867 and afterward devoted his energies to vigorously promoting mass transit in New York.

His efforts finally were successful. Construction of the Gilbert Elevated Railroad began in 1876 but was quickly halted by the legal maneuvers of a rather considerable opposition of property owners and horsecar lines. The February 9, 1878, issue of *Harper's Weekly,* commented on this:

> The opposition encountered by the elevated roads from property holders, as well as from the horse-car companies, was quite natural. It can not be pleasant to have trains of cars whizzing by one's second-story windows every five minutes, even though the rate of speed precludes a too curious scrutiny of private apartments; and it must be confessed that the tracks, whether on the line of the sidewalks or over the roadway, do not improve the appearance of a street. But private objections and individual convenience must always yield when they stand in the way of the greatest good of the greatest number; and the grievances of the few are nothing when weighed in the balance with the vast benefits which thousands upon thousands of people will derive from the completion of these lines.

The legal barriers were overcome by October 1877, and construction immediately resumed. The original Gilbert line ran from the Battery to Central Park, mainly along Sixth Avenue. The February 9, 1878, issue of *Harper's Weekly* indicated stations were to be built at 52nd Street, 42nd Street, 34th Street, 23rd Street, 14th Street, Clinton Place, Bleecker Street, Grand Street, Franklin Street, Chambers Street, Park Place, Morris Street, and Cortlandt or Liberty Streets. As a way of extending this road around Central Park, a line was built along 52nd Street from Sixth Avenue to Ninth Avenue. There it shared the New York Elevated Railroad line as far as its terminus at 59th Street, and then continued on to 110th Street, only to turn east to Eighth Avenue, where it then extended on north to Harlem.

Both railroads also had begun constructing East Side lines. The June 15, 1878, issue of *Scientific American* observed:

> When the elevated railways, now in progress of construction in this city, are completed, four great iron bridges will run lengthwise over Manhattan Island. When finished they will aggregate in length between sixty and seventy miles and there will be two on each side of the city. On the East Side, the New York Elevated Road runs a double track from White-Hall through Front and Pearl streets, Bowery, and Third Avenue to the end of the island at Harlem. The Gilbert Elevated Road has a circuitous route from Bowling Green to Second Avenue, and along the latter street to Harlem, where it traverses the island over to Eighth Avenue.

In May 1879 both the Gilbert Elevated Railroad (which by this time had become the Metropolitan Elevated Railroad) and the New York Elevated Railroad companies were leased to the Manhattan Company and were operated under one directorship. Under this system lines were merged in some instances and new extensions were made.

Following the lead of Manhattan, Brooklyn began its own elevated railroads, building three of them from the mid- to late 1880s. The Brooklyn Elevated Railroad was inaugurated on May 13, 1885. The Union Elevated Railroad ran parallel to part of the Brooklyn Elevated Railroad and the lines were merged in the 1890s. The King's County Elevated Railroad ran from the Fulton Ferry (across from Fulton Street, Manhattan) to Bedford, then extended to Stuyvesant Heights, and later to East New York.

Chicago also inaugurated its own elevated system in 1895. More than a decade earlier, however, the Illinois Central established itself as a city railroad, setting up numerous stops along its route near the lake shore. It built separate tracks for its city and suburban traffic, added special equipment, and ran trains at short intervals. Small steam locomotives, typically Forney types, were in general use on elevated lines. However, beginning with Daft's experiments in 1888, plans were made for electrification. In 1897 the nation's first subway system, using trolleys, began operation underneath Tremont Street in Boston. The invention of the multiple-unit control system by Frank J. Sprague, allowing a single motorman to control a number of electrified cars as one train, was a breakthrough occurring before Brooklyn's lines were electrified in 1901 and Manhattan's in 1902. The long-dreamed-of subway for Manhattan finally became a reality as ground was broken on the Interborough Rapid Transit (IRT) line in early 1900. The inauguration of its first nine miles occurred on October 27, 1904.

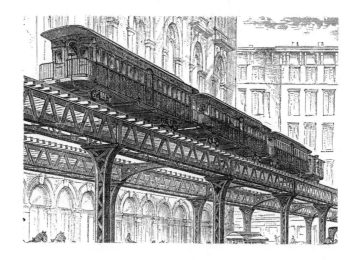

Top; Deitz's proposed railway for Broadway, 1853. Bottom; Swett's proposed elevated railway for Broadway, 1853.

Left; Wickersham's proposed railroad terrace for Broadway, 1854. Right; Andrew's proposed elevated railroad for Broadway, 1865.

Top; "The proposed Broadway Railroad—The bridge elevations at the street crossings," 1866. Bottom; Experimental elevated railway on Greenwich St., 1868 [This later evolved into the New York Elevated R.R. 9th Ave. line].

A proposed underground railway for Broadway, 1867.

A pneumatic elevated railway for city transit, proposed by Dr. Rufus H. Gilbert, 1871.

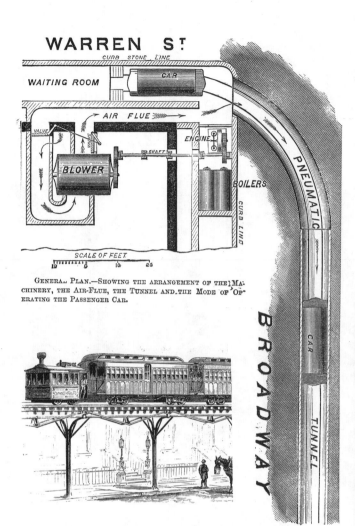

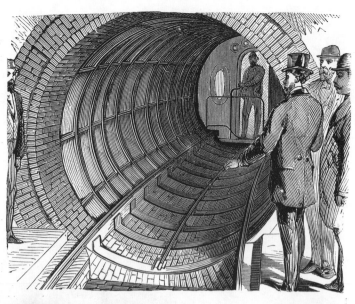

Top left, top right, and middle right; The Broadway Pneumatic Underground Railway, 1872: Top left; General plan. Top right; Portal of the Broadway tunnel. Middle right; Interior of pneumatic passenger car. Middle left; Train of Gilbert Elevated R.R., 1878. Bottom; Station design for proposed Broadway underground railway, 1876.

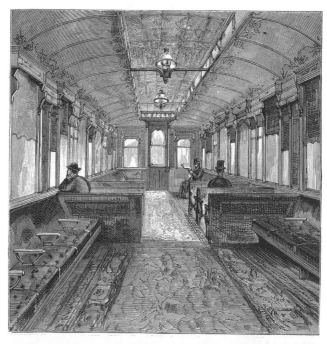

The Gilbert Elevated Railroad [later Metropolitan Elevated R.R.], May, 1878. Top left; Exterior of car. Top right; Interior of car. Bottom; Raising cars upon the track over an inclined plane.

Top left; Station on 9th Ave. and 42nd St., New York Elevated R.R., Feb. 1878. Top right; Train of Gilbert Elevated R.R., c.1878. Bottom; Scene on 6th Ave. near 34th St., Gilbert Elevated R.R., Feb. 1878.

Railroad construction on New Church St. [Trinity Church in background], Gilbert Elevated R.R., May, 1878.

Scene in Greenwich Village on 6th Ave. [Jefferson Courthouse in background], Gilbert Elevated R.R., May 1878.

Top left; Station at 4th Ave. and 42nd St. [Grand Central Station in background], New York Elevated R.R., east side line, Sept. 1878. Top right; Dr. Rufus H. Gilbert, longtime promoter of mass transit in New York. Bottom; Station at 6th Ave. and 42nd St., Metropolitan Elevated R.R., July 1878.

Scene in Franklin Square [Hanover Square Station at top], New York Elevated R.R., east side line, Sept. 1878.

Top; Crossing of New York and Metropolitan Elevated railroads at Pearl, Wall and Beaver Sts., Mar. 1879. Bottom; Station at Bowery and Grand Sts., New York Elevated R.R., east side line, 1879.

Top; Head-on train collision on east side line near 42nd St., New York Elevated R.R., Mar. 25, 1879. Bottom; Train on east side line, New York Elevated R.R., 1879.

Extension of Metropolitan Elevated R.R., looking north from 110th St. at 8th Ave., Nov. 1879.

The 9th Ave. line: Left; Looking south from 81st St., Aug. 1879. Right; A station on the line, 1885.

Accident at 145th St. and 8th Ave., when late hour train carrying off work rail employees hits unexpected switch while going too fast, Metropolitan Elevated R.R., Feb. 1880. Top left; Switchman vainly trying to stop train. Top right; Removing engineer, fireman, and conductor from car. Bottom; Wreckage of "dummy" locomotive.

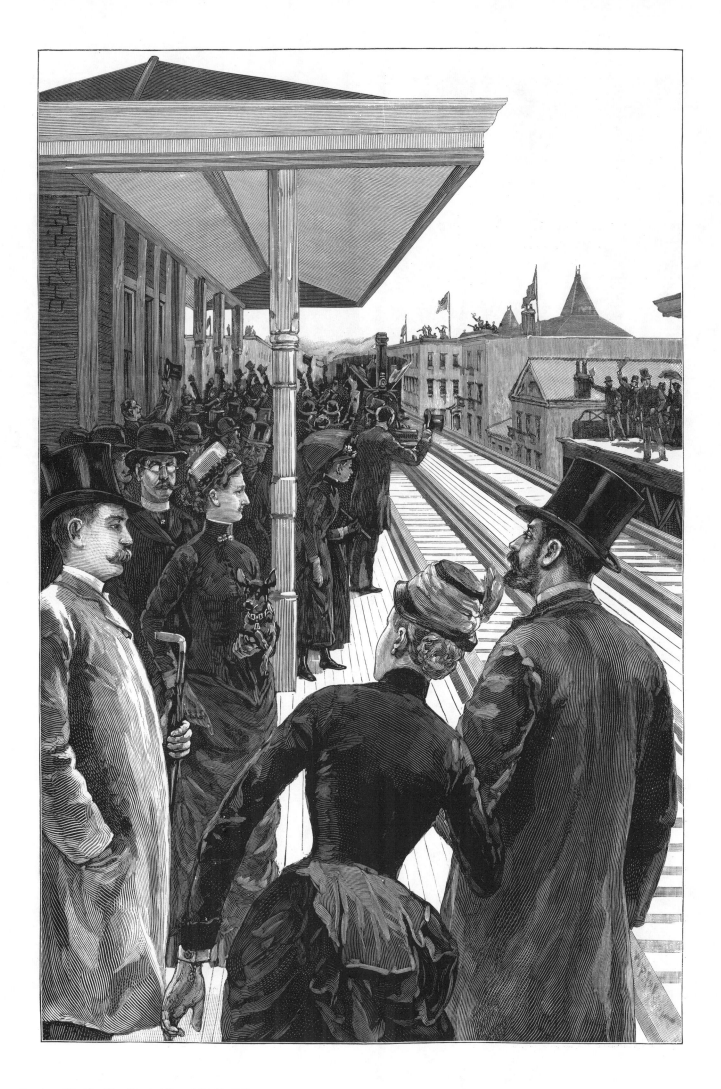

Opening of the Brooklyn Elevated Rwy., May 13, 1885.

"A bitter night at an elevated railroad station," Feb. 1887.

A preview of future electrification: Daft electric locomotive making trial run on 9th Ave. section of Metropolitan Elevated R.R., late 1888.

"A station scene in the rush hours on the Manhattan Elevated Railroad," Feb. 1890.

BIBLIOGRAPHY

In addition to the original source material used in writing the introductory texts for this volume, the following books have also been consulted.

Beebe, Lucius, and Charles Clegg. *Hear the Train Blow: A Pictorial Epic of America in the Railroad Age.* New York: E. P. Dutton, 1952.

Douglas, George H. *All Aboard: The Railroad in American Life.* New York: Paragon House, 1992.

Fletcher, Malcolm, and John Taylor. *Railways: The Pioneer Years.* Secaucus, N.J.: Chartwell Books, 1990.

Frey, Robert L., editor. *Encyclopedia of American Business History: Railroads in the Nineteenth Century.* New York: Facts on File Publications, 1988.

Hornung, Clarence P. *Wheels Across America.* New York: A. S. Barnes and Co., 1959.

Hubbard, Freeman. *Encyclopedia of North American Railroading.* New York: McGraw-Hill, 1981.

Hungerford, Edward. *Locomotives on Parade.* New York: Thomas Y. Crowell, 1940.

Jensen, Oliver. *The American Heritage History of Railroads in America.* New York: American Heritage, 1975.

Loco Profile #11: The Norris Locomotives. Windsor, Berkshire, England: Profile Publications, 1971.

Reed, Robert C. *Train Wrecks: A Pictorial History of Accidents on the Main Line.* New York: Bonanza Books, 1968.

Rowsome, Frank. *Trolley Car Treasury.* New York: Bonanza Books, 1956.

Turner, George Edgar. *Victory Rode the Rails: The Strategic Place of the Railroads in the Civil War.* Indianapolis and New York: Bobbs-Merrill, 1953.

White, John H., Jr. *The American Railroad Freight Car.* Baltimore: John Hopkins University Press, 1993.